D0031337

WHAT OTHERS ARE SAYING

Many of those who write about faith have an idealized version of faith in mind, which they describe in cliché-ridden language that makes those Christians who do not experience such faith feel either guilty or angry. In *The Grand Paradox*, Ken Wytsma talks about actual faith, not idealized faith. The faith of which he speaks is not only *for* our messy world but also *of* our messy world—while yet trusting and revealing God. Thoroughly honest, never evasive, free of clichés, deeply Christian, encouraging rather than scolding in its tone, it is the most perceptive and helpful discussion of faith that I know of.

—NICHOLAS WOLTERSTORFF, NOAH PORTER
PROFESSOR EMERITUS OF PHILOSOPHICAL
THEOLOGY, YALE UNIVERSITY, SENIOR RESEARCH
FELLOW, INSTITUTE FOR ADVANCED STUDIES IN
CULTURE, UNIVERSITY OF VIRGINIA

With refreshing honesty, Ken explores our journey toward *real* faith, the kind that sustains us through seasons of suffering and strengthens us through life's mysteries. Deeply personal, yet anchored biblically, *The Grand Paradox* will both encourage and energize you. I commend it highly.

—STEPHAN BAUMAN, PRESIDENT
AND CEO OF WORLD RELIEF

The Grand Paradox will change your vision and create a "new normal" as a guide for pursuing God. Read this book, and then tell everyone about it.

—JOHN SOWERS, PRESIDENT OF THE MENTORING
PROJECT AND AUTHOR OF *FATHERLESS
GENERATION* AND *THE HEROIC PATH*

Honest, compelling, and filled with Scripture, *The Grand Paradox* invites you to a deeper life of love, justice, and mercy in the midst of brokenness and pain. Ken's latest book will help you hold onto hope as you live and serve.

—PETER GREER, PRESIDENT AND CEO OF HOPE
INTERNATIONAL AND COAUTHOR OF *MISSION DRIFT*
AND *THE SPIRITUAL DANGER OF DOING GOOD*

Far too many of us today despise paradox and avoid the tensions that exist naturally in our lives and world and faith. Ken Wytsma's brilliant and wide-ranging book does a bold and masterful job of inviting us straight into the heart of the grand paradoxes God has woven into the fabric of the universe. Under Wytsma's wise guidance, we begin to see that the life of faith is a leap INTO paradox, not OUT of it. This book is a tour de force of good stories, philosophical wisdom, and theological insight, potent enough to realign many of our most egregious misunderstandings, enlightening enough to help us begin to see more clearly, hope-filled enough to help us to live more faithfully and flourishingly.

—MICHAEL YANKOSKI, AUTHOR OF *THE SACRED YEAR* AND *UNDER THE OVERPASS*

This book forced me to don my thinking cap. It also made me laugh, loudly. Who else but author Ken Wytsma comes away from lunch at In-N-Out Burger intent on a Southern California prayer fast? *The Grand Paradox* is not a book for readers looking for a four-step plan to a happy-sappy faith. *The Grand Paradox* is for readers whose lives are a hot mess. If you have ever wondered if God is a psychotic hiding behind black velvet drapes, orchestrating the chaos that is your life, read this book. *The Grand Paradox* won't provide easy answers, but it is sure to help readers frame faith around the most important of questions.

—KAREN SPEARS ZACHARIAS, AUTHOR OF *MOTHER OF RAIN*

Some books can be read and digested reasonably well by yourself. Other books, however, are so stimulating and provocative they should also be read in community. I believe *The Grand Paradox* is in the latter category. Ken Wytsma treats "the messiness of life and the mysteriousness of God and His ways" in a candid, constructive, and compelling manner. So get a group of friends and read it together. I'm confident that you will be blessed, and so will they!

—RANDAL ROBERTS, D.MIN., PRESIDENT, WESTERN SEMINARY (PORTLAND, OR)

Question: What do Soren Kierkegaard, C. S. Lewis, Abraham Heschel, Dwight Moody, Dietrich Bonhoeffer, Reinhold Niebuhr, Evelyn Underhill, and John Paul II all have in common? Answer: They all make an appearance in and contribute to the present book by Ken Wytsma. Wytsma has taken many rich voices of the Christian tradition and has processed them through his well-informed passionate faith with a keen eye on the practical consequences of such faith for life in the world. Wytsma connects the dots between tradition, faith, and practice in a compelling way that readers will find fresh and enlivening.

—WALTER BRUEGGEMANN, COLUMBIA
THEOLOGICAL SEMINARY

Paradox is central to life with Jesus: die to live; serve to gain; weakness is strength. In an age that idolizes certainty over mystery and skepticism over trust, many assume our doubts oppose faith. Wytsma powerfully reclaims the ancient truth, rather, that doubt is the context in which faith can arise, paradox the soil in which trust grows. With pastoral sensitivity for our heartrending questions—like "Where is God?" when life is tragic, or "What is God's will?" when the road is messy—Wytsma helps us weary, war-torn travelers pull the cynicism and despair out of our modern backpacks and trade them in for joy in a God who is mysteriously present—not in spite of our troubles, but through them—and who is faithful and reliable to make our world right.

—JOSHUA RYAN BUTLER, PASTOR AND AUTHOR
OF *THE SKELETONS IN GOD'S CLOSET*

Ken engages in the complexities rather than celebrates the simplicities of a life of faith, reminding us that the Christian life is non-linear and that it is when we engage in deeper dialogue that the messiness of faith is revealed and space for raw and honest conversation takes place. Through Scripture, reflection, and questions Ken emphasizes that what may feel messy is often what's required, and necessary, for a life of faith. *The Grand Paradox* reminds us to engage in the messy, to embrace it as something beautiful, and I hope that every church and follower of Jesus reads this.

—RACHEL GOBLE, PRESIDENT
OF THE SOLD PROJECT

The most important thing Ken Wytsma has done is listen. He has listened to the voices of our fast-paced, noisy culture, and he has listened to the God who desperately wants to redeem it. He has a fire in his bones that has sparked from the urgency that comes from reading the Bible in one hand and the newspaper in the other. Now he is speaking and writing and organizing the things he has heard. Like a growing number of Christians, Ken is convinced that our faith is not just a ticket into heaven and a license to ignore the world around us. His latest book is a paradigm-changer inspiring us to take risks, obey God's leading in radical ways, pray without ceasing, love those on the margins, and find our ultimate happiness in giving our lives away. Ken is in love with Jesus, he is a man of prayer, and in *The Grand Paradox* he leads us deeper into the beauty and mystery of the Christian life. One of the most thought-provoking books on faith to come out in a long time.

—SHANE CLAIBORNE, AUTHOR,
ACTIVIST, AND FRIEND OF KEN WYTSMA

Ken Wytsma's *The Grand Paradox* is a wonderful book. It captures the adventure, the mystery, and the sheer risk of life with God, and moves beyond the clichés of modern Christianity into something much deeper and more beautiful. Ken perfectly captures the joys and trials of faith. I highly recommend this book!

—MIKE ERRE, LEAD PASTOR OF EV FREE
FULLERTON AND AUTHOR OF *ASTONISHED*
AND *WHY THE BIBLE MATTERS*

In *The Grand Paradox*, Ken Wytsma dives into the many parodoxes of the Kingdom of God, where the first are last, the weak are strong, and a peasant child becomes King. Instead of underplaying tensions, he unpacks them with profound simplicity and aptly demonstrates that Christianity's seeming contradictions are the crux of our faith and the source of its mystery—like the two intersecting beams of Christ's cross. This book gave me new eyes to appreciate the grand paradoxes of heaven and earth, deity and humanity, joy and sorrow, faith and doubt, now and forever.

—SARAH THEBARGE, AUTHOR
OF *THE INVISIBLE GIRLS*

In *The Grand Paradox* we see Ken doing what he is best at. He knocks the false security of religion out from under us and replaces it with God's humbling invitation to us: to live in the messy tension between what we want and what God wants for us, between suffering and blessing, between injustice and perfection, between hopelessness and certainty. In the radical middle we find the life-giving Christ. This is one of the most comprehensive and engaging books on Christian faith available today.

—RICK MCKINLEY, LEAD PASTOR OF IMAGO DEI
COMMUNITY, AUTHOR OF *THE ANSWER TO OUR
CRY* AND *THIS BEAUTIFUL MESS*

For many the world may be a contradiction, our universe a paradox, but Ken Wytsma reveals our greatest of joy is found in our hope in God and how our faith in Him helps us experience His faithfulness and love for us.

—MATT KNISELY, EMMY AWARD-
WINNING PHOTOJOURNALIST AND
AUTHOR OF *FRAMING FAITH*

In *The Grand Paradox*, Ken Wytsma delivers an honest, thoughtful, and thoroughly biblical primer on the messiness of living by faith in a mysterious God. This book isn't about easy answers; it's about the art of struggling forward as we follow the Savior in spite of our unanswered questions. This book will mark your thoughts in ways that please Jesus and will become a valued resource in the future.

—Ed Underwood, Pastor of Church of
the Open Door, Author of *When God
Breaks Your Heart* and *The Trail*

In his latest book, Ken Wytsma wrestles wisely with faith's most profound questions. Is faith the opposite of knowing and evidence? How can I believe when things are so painful, complicated, and chaotic? Yes, faith is entrusting my whole life and way of living to what God says is true. But there are so many places where God and His way are wrapped in mystery. Is suffering the shoal or school of our faith? How does faith relate to doubt and wonder, to pain, deep fatigue, and doing what is always right? What does faith look like in a culture of fast-moving conversations, unlimited possibility, and the peeping voyeurism of online life? How can faith lead to hope, happiness, and blessing especially when they are slow coming? In the end, Ken shows how faith is a beautifully awkward reality lived in this messy middle-Gethsemane world between the gardens of Eden and Zion. *The Grand Paradox* is a great help to praying "God come near" as we leap into trust.

—Gerry Breshears, PhD,
Professor of Theology,
Western Seminary, Portland

Ken is a historian and theologian who also has the heart of a pastor. He gently walks us through places in *The Grand Paradox* that are hard, yet necessary, as believers. This book does three things: it challenges our paradigms through great theological ideas, it inspires us to keep going as believers, and it confronts us with the need to examine our faith—all the while assuring us God loves us. There are very few books or authors who can accomplish all three like Ken does in *The Grand Paradox*. My head and heart were full after engaging this book. I hope yours will be as well.

—Leroy Barber, Author of
Everyday Missions and *Red, Brown,
Yellow, Black, White—Who's More
Precious in God's Sight?*

I read this book during a somewhat vulnerable time in my life, and it rolled around in my head for a long while afterward because it gifted me a strange peace with so many of my questions—not by giving black-and-white answers, but by reminding me that God rarely gives them in the first place. I've been a Christian most of my life, and yet the older I get, the less sure I am of anything beyond God's beloved son Jesus and his deep love for all of humanity. Ken's book is a significant voice of clarity for people on a faith journey whose path is riddled with fog. Enthusiastic applause for this gem.

—Tsh Oxenreider, Author of Notes
from a Blue Bike: The Art of Living
Intentionally in a Chaotic World

THE GRAND
PARADOX

THE GRAND
PARADOX

The Messiness of Life, the Mystery of God
and the *Necessity* of Faith

KEN WYTSMA

W PUBLISHING GROUP

AN IMPRINT OF THOMAS NELSON

Published in Nashville, Tennessee, by W Publishing, an imprint of Thomas Nelson.

Published in association with the literary agency of D.C. Jacobson & Associates, LLC, an Author Management Company, www.dcjacobson.com.

Thomas Nelson titles may be purchased in bulk for educational, business, fund-raising, or sales promotional use. For information, please e-mail SpecialMarkets@ThomasNelson.com.

ISBN: 978-0-7180-3139-8 (ITPE)

Library of Congress Cataloging-in-Publication Data

Wytsma, Ken.
  The grand paradox : the messiness of life, the mystery of God, and the necessity of faith / Ken Wytsma.
    pages cm
  ISBN 978-0-8499-6467-1 (hardcover)
  1. Christian life. 2. Life--Religious aspects--Christianity. 3. Christianity--Philosophy. I. Title.
  BV4501.3.W97 2015
  248.4--dc23

                      2014022312

Printed in the United States of America

14 15 16 17 18 RRD 6 5 4 3 2 1

To my daughters,
Mary Joy, Esther, Sara, and Ashlin.
Your dad loves you.

Paradox simply means a certain defiant joy which belongs to belief.[1]

—G. K. CHESTERTON

CONTENTS

CONTENTS

FOREWORD

One of the most disturbing *and* fascinating stories in the Scriptures—at least for me—comes from Mark 4:35–41. It's a dramatic, life-and-death story. It's a story that involves Jesus, the disciples, a boat, and what was meant to be a smooth and safe journey across the Sea of Galilee.

Many may be familiar with this story but it was only later in my life, in a closer examination of this tale, I realized this harrowing near-death experience began with Jesus saying, "Let's get to the other side of the lake." In other words, Jesus initiates this trip. Did you get that?

Jesus initiates this life-and-death episode.

This is why the story is so disturbing . . . because at the core, it contradicts so much of what we want to believe about faith in God and what it means to be a follower of Christ:

Just believe in Jesus and everything will be perfect. (Or pretty darn close.)

Health. Wealth. Blessings. Prosperity.

Enjoy. Give God the glory. Repeat.

This is what I learned, or selectively learned, and wanted to believe.

What inevitably happens is that we try to figure out the magic spiritual formula. We try to figure out God and make absolute sense of faith. We make plans and set the course for our life journeys. We create Excel sheets of our hopes, plans, and ambitions. We leave no room for mystery, and thus, can't make any sense of doubt, confusion, and questions.

And this is where *The Grand Paradox: The Messiness of Life, the Mystery of God and the Necessity of Faith* comes in. To call this a great book would not be an appropriate way to describe the hope and vision behind the book. We all know that there are books out there that give us ninety-nine steps for this, forty days for that, seven ways for farther here, or three steps for deeper there.

This kind of nicely-packaged formula sells because well, there's a market for such nicely-packaged formulas. We yearn for our lives and our world to be neatly seasoned for our appetites and our desires for order and dare I say, *control*. Yes, we even want our God to fit nicely in our compartments, categories, and boxes for us to fully understand and perhaps, even manipulate.

Ken Wytsma doesn't provide easy steps, pat answers, or a systematic approach. If that's what you're looking for, keep looking. It's not convenient or palatable. It's not a book that gives you clear directions—like a step-by-step spiritual GPS.

No, it's not that kind of book.

What kind of book is this? It's a gut check. An honest look in the mirror. It's one of those books that says, "Whatever. Let's just try to put everything on the table . . . knowing that the table will still be messy when it's done."

The Grand Paradox is both refreshing and uncomfortably honest. Any book where the author (who happens to be a pastor among other things) openly confesses that he sometimes "falls asleep during other people's lengthy, verbose prayers, or who begins to think about football or movies" . . . is gutsy (or insane). I'm also a pastor and during prayer time, I am only deeply immersed in prayer, faith, God, Jesus, the Holy Spirit, the Kingdom of God, and the Holy Scriptures [*cough, cough*]. Yes, only these things. All the time.

No, it's not *that* kind of book.

And this is good.

Not only is it good but it's very important.

It's important because there are dangers to a false, glamorous, and unrealistic perception of what it means to have faith in God and be a follower of Christ. A spirituality that leaves no room for doubts, questions, and messiness will inevitably lead to dire consequences. A false allusion of faith and discipleship sets up people for epic failures, bouts with disillusionment, and at times, a slow but sinking spiral into cynicism.

What we need today isn't more formulaic how-tos from self-professing gurus. We don't need more dazzling storytellers, we need more genuine storytellers. Ken reminds us in *The Grand Paradox* that doubt is not the enemy of faith and that mystery is not to be feared. Even doubt and mystery—like the fierce winds and chaotic sea—submit to Christ.

In that near-death sea story, I should explain that many of the disciples were professional fishermen. They fished that Sea of Galilee hundreds if not thousands of times. They were experts and the truth is they would have never set sail if they knew danger was imminent.

Such are our lives. Such are our hearts and minds. Such are our goals. We try to understand the mysteries of life. We try to comprehend and analyze the profundity of the God of the cosmos. We pride ourselves in becoming experts and being captains of our own lives, circumstances, and world until we realize that no matter how much we've charted the seas, we never have full control of our lives or the seas.

The hope of the gospel is not that God promises us health, wealth, and a life full of bliss and perfection, but that God is with us—through all circumstances. God is present in our mountaintops and valleys . . . and everything in between. God is present in the tranquility of calm seas and the ferocity of our chaotic circumstances. And God is present even—and especially—in our doubts, pain, and mess.

I'm fascinated by this story of Jesus, the disciples, and their journey across the Sea of Galilee. The disciples feared for their lives. They even wondered and openly questioned how Jesus could be sleeping during such an occasion. But we have to be minded that Jesus never promised a quick, easy, and straight journey. Jesus never promised a smooth sail on a decked-out yacht. He does promise one thing: "Let's get to the other side of the lake."

And if Christ promises to get us to the other side of the lake, He'll get us to the other side. Mess, doubts, pain, tension, and all.

Thanks Ken for reminding us to be deeply honest about the messiness of life and, in spite of it all and even because of it all, to place our faith in the One who meets us in our mess and continues to pursue us.

—Eugene Cho

Pastor of Quest Church and Founder of

One Day's Wages

Author of *Overrated: Are We More in Love with the Idea of Changing the World Than Actually Changing the World?*

INTRODUCTION

This Beautiful Mess

We want answers from God. We have a ravenous appetite for clarity in life. And often, we desire justification or, at least, some kind of explanation for why He allows certain things to transpire. God, however, is more mysterious than we think He should be or wish He were. Most of the time, we don't receive the desired answers or the clarity for which we clamor. In spite of our seeking, God seems just out of our reach. Try as we might, we cannot pin Him down.

In short, the truth is: life is messy, and God is mysterious.

We struggle with these truths. We spend our energy, often wrestling in prayer, hoping to attain that place of peace in which our life is less difficult, painful, and challenging.

Yet the messiness of life remains a constant reality, and God remains mysterious.

Life is messy and God is mysterious. I first heard it expressed this way by my fellow pastor, Bud Burk, as he summarized his extensive interaction with the writings of Eugene Peterson. For me, the statement accurately captures the tension of faith. We even find this tension echoed in the teaching of Jesus: while we desire simple formulas, Jesus taught in apparent riddles.

So how do we live, grow, flourish, and remain content in the mess? How do we trust, follow, and continue to obey God when He seems to remain elusive?

Several years into my Christian walk, I was the pastor of a large college group while taking a heavy load of graduate classes in philosophy. I was overwhelmed. I didn't have enough time. I was out of money. I couldn't clearly see the path for the next steps in life.

I was giving my life to God, I thought, so why was everything so difficult and confusing?

I found myself caught in this awkward middle—the place between my belief about how things ought to be and the reality of how they actually were; between how I thought God should move in my life and how He actually chose to move.

And this is when I began to realize: *faith is often characterized less by clarity than by confusion.*

We all long for a sense of God's will for our lives, for intimacy with God, and for the presence and power of the Holy Spirit. We desire God's love and affection. As hard as it is to accept for most of us, these things will come at the back end of a long walk of faith, or, to borrow a phrase from Friedrich Nietzsche, "a long obedience in the same direction."

In the meantime, though, the questions remain: What is God's will for my life? What is faith? What does it mean to follow, to know, to experience God? How do we find the right path, discover who we were created to be, know what it is we are called to do? And why can it seem so hard?

If we were made for relationship with God, why do we often feel lost and distant from Him? When we, who call ourselves followers of Jesus, feel as if we're groping blindly, have we missed some key concept or failed to grasp the correct formula?

The life of Christian faith is and always has been a beautifully awkward reality. Following Jesus is done—can only be done—in the messiness of this world into which we were all born. Yet many Christians expect the walk of faith to be easier, neater, and relatively devoid of hassles.

So perhaps it's time for a frank conversation about the true nature of Christian faith. Maybe there are many desperately in need of a clear dialogue about how—despite living in a turbulent, chaotic world—our greatest joy is found in our pursuit of God.

This book is an exploration of the art of living by faith. It is a book for all those wrestling with the paradoxes that confront those who seek to walk with Christ. It is a look at how faith works, here and now, in our culture, our time—and how to put down real roots and flourish in the midst of our messy lives.

As we explore together the mysterious nature of our relationship with God, may we find joy. May we come to experience the full measure of God's faithfulness and love for us.

Ken Wytsma
Bend, Oregon

JERICHO

I find that doing the will of God leaves me no
time for disputing about His plans.[1]
—George MacDonald

Throughout history, the Old City of Jerusalem has been viewed as the heart
of the world. Today as you leave the Old City and drive east on the winding
Highway 1, you begin a dramatic descent from the hill country into the
desert. The change in elevation has a significant effect on weather conditions, creating a visible distinction between the lush, green Jerusalem to the
west and the severe, dusty, desert climate of the West Bank to the east. The
change in vegetation is so drastic that it can be seen from satellites in space.

As you enter this desert, where Bedouin shepherds have roamed for
thousands of years, you soon come across the security checkpoint separating Israel from the West Bank. As you enter Area A of the West Bank, an
area under full Palestinian control, a red sign forbids entrance to Israelis at
the risk of death. Here Highway 1 joins the historic Jericho Road.

Continuing on, you enter the Jordan Rift Valley. The Jordan Rift is distinct but connected to the Great Rift Valley that extends all the way from Mozambique through Egypt and reaches its lowest point at the Dead Sea. Just eleven miles from Jerusalem you'll pass an archaeological site of a hostel halfway between Jerusalem and Jericho. Tradition says it is the inn where the parable of the good Samaritan took place, and hence is named the Inn of the Good Samaritan.

Another fourteen miles from there, in an oasis of the Jordan Valley, lie the ancient ruins of what is said to be the oldest continually inhabited city in the world—the city of Jericho.[2]

This area, a part of the larger Judean wilderness, is characterized by rugged terrain that offered safe hiding for rebels, bandits, and outcasts in ancient times. The first inhabitants were nomads who transitioned from the hunter-gatherer lifestyle among the caves and hills to a city-dwelling society, as agriculture was made possible by the proximity of the Jericho oasis.[3] With a warm climate year-round and natural springwater irrigation allowing for lush agriculture, "the city of palm trees"[4] was in a desirable location worth settling in and certainly worth protecting.

Historically, Jericho was a walled city known throughout antiquity for its defensive capability.[5] If you go there now and walk to the middle of the mound where there has been extensive excavation since the early 1900s, you can look over the ledge and see an exposed portion of one of the original towers of Jericho that dates back to the Neolithic period.[6] The tower is said to be the oldest stone-built structure of its kind in the world.[7]

Jericho is mentioned fifty-nine times in Scripture. It was the city of refuge where David told his servants to stay until their beards grew back, after they were publicly humiliated by the Ammonite king.[8] Jesus healed the blind man Bartimaeus along the roadside outside of the city,[9] and it was in Jericho that Zacchaeus climbed up into the sycamore tree in an attempt to see Christ.[10] There's an old sycamore tree in the center of town today that tourists visit, and many believe it is the one Zacchaeus climbed.

But the most prominent and important narrative associated with Jericho deals with the events leading up to and immediately following its conquest by the Israelites under Joshua.[11] It is not only a history with significance for the people of Israel; it also offers profound lessons for the church and for every believer who is moving forward in faith toward the calling God has given.

As a foundation for *The Grand Paradox*, we can look at the events surrounding Joshua and Jericho. Before we can discuss the many aspects of walking by faith, we need to ground ourselves in the very same lessons that God took such pains to teach Joshua and the generation of Israelites that were with him at Jericho.

JERICHO FALLS

After forty years of wandering, Moses died and leadership was passed to Joshua. God gave Joshua very specific instructions about how the Jordan River crossing was to take place. The priests bearing the ark of the covenant were to lead the crossing, thus demonstrating to everyone that the presence of the Lord of all the earth was to go first.[12]

After the entire camp crossed the river, men from each tribe were sent back with instructions to retrieve twelve large stones from the riverbed to be piled up and to serve as a memorial; the people were commanded to never forget the miracle—of holding back the Jordan River waters—God performed that day and to tell it to their children for generations to come.[13]

Rather than rushing into the military campaign, God took the time to illustrate something important to His people: He goes first, and they are to follow.

He leads, and *we* follow.

• • •

Upon crossing the Jordan, the Israelites renewed their covenant vows of obedience to God, spending their first weeks in the promised land realigning their relationship with Him. They were ready to take the land, starting with the city of Jericho. But Joshua was about to undergo a dramatic course correction.[14] An angel with an unsheathed sword appeared to Joshua just outside Jericho. Apparently that wasn't enough to intimidate Joshua, so he challenged, "Whose side are you on: ours or our enemies'?"

But Joshua was missing the point. The angel responded, "Neither . . . but as commander of the army of the LORD I have now come" (Joshua 5:14). And Joshua fell to his face in reverence.

Engrossed in the stress and sweat of planning the first military conquest in the promised land, Joshua was literally brought to his knees by God's reminder that it wasn't his battle. Likewise, any of us can forget that we are part of a bigger narrative. We can easily fall prey to stress, pain, or pressure, allowing obstacles to loom larger in our vision than the God who is trying to lead us. We are reminded through Joshua's example: the battle is the Lord's.

• • •

Israel's soldiers gathered to hear the plan. Their courageous leader delivered the brilliant strategy: March in circles around the city for seven days. Blow horns, make music, and yell. Wait for the walls to collapse.[15]

I doubt the plan was received well. This is not a brilliant military strategy; this is a death wish. The city of Jericho was well fortified and difficult to assault.

Yet, instead of relying on human strength and ability, Joshua gambled on obedience and trust in God, and the walls fell on the seventh day.

There is no question about the source of the victory. God went to great lengths to show Joshua and the Israelites whose battle it was. He has sent the message over and over—"This enterprise is Mine, not yours."

• • •

As the Israelites invaded Jericho, God gave them specific instructions to set aside any precious metals among the spoils as a sacrifice to Him. Everything else was to be destroyed.

"But the Israelites were unfaithful in regard to the devoted things."[16]

One man in particular, Achan, did not trust in the goodness of God's commands.[17] He was overtaken by greed. He began to rationalize his desires, and in the end, he chose to ignore God's command, break the covenant, and keep some of the spoil. He took what he saw—put himself at the center and pushed God out to the margins.

This one seemingly small slip of individualism and greed caused a domino effect of pain and suffering for Achan, his family, and the entire army of Israel.

The covenant was broken and God's anger burned against the nation.

We're not much different from Achan. We labor and contrive, grounding our plans in our own reason and intellect, our own sense of entitlement. We struggle with our greed and desires. We want to pocket more stuff. After all, we have earned it, haven't we?

But that's not how it's supposed to be.

THE LORD AT THE CENTER

It is God who goes first, and as He leads, we follow. We stand on God's side—not Him on ours. God razes the walls; only in His strength do we find victory.

As with Joshua and all God's children, we need to acknowledge that He demands the place of primacy in our lives—in our communities, our conquests, our achievements, our thoughts and desires.

This message—that the Lord is at the center—reverberates throughout Scripture, from the account of Jericho to the narratives of the judges, the kings, and the exile. When the Lord was placed at the center, the people flourished and were blessed; whenever they turned their backs on Him, they experienced defeat, turmoil, slavery, and exile.

We find the same message in imperative form in the Ten Commandments delivered a generation earlier to Moses. Of the ten, the first three deal with the centrality of God.[18]

This theme is delivered poetically in numerous psalms and proverbs, such as Psalm 111:10, "The fear of the LORD is the beginning of wisdom" (KJV).

Even the name of the lead character in the Jericho account teaches a lesson. The Hebrew name Joshua literally means, "The Lord is salvation."[19] And as the metanarrative of scripture rolls on, we see this same message in the person of Christ. From the Hebrew name Joshua comes the Greek name Jesus—the One who is our salvation.

In the end, as Paul penned in Romans 11:36: "For from him and through him and to him are all things."

For much of history, Christians have seen the crucifixion as humanity's crucial moment. Christ's death and resurrection are the most important events not only in church history, but in all of human history. (As a side note, *crucifixion*, *crux*, and *crucial* share the same Latin root, all pointing to the idea of a cross.)

All scripture points to one thing: life is about God. The process of moving from confused wandering to purpose and joy is marked by faith, by waiting on the Lord in ready obedience.

Recently, my wife, Tamara, and I circled up with our four girls for bedtime prayers. As is the norm, I asked the girls what they were thankful for, and then proceeded to see who would be willing to pray for the family.

Our youngest, Ashlin, who was a week away from five years old enthusiastically asked to pray. We all smiled and waited for her to begin.

She started off in a loud and happy voice: "I'm thank you for my sister Mary Joy. I'm thank you for my sister Esther. I'm thank you for my sister Sara. I'm thank you for my mommy, Mommy. And I'm thank you for my daddy, Daddy."

It was hard to keep her sisters from giggling, but we all appreciated her words and heart enough to keep the chuckles in and allow her to finish as she "thank-you'd" God for the rest of our family and church.

Her transposition of *thankful* into *thank you* seemed like an innocent and sincere slip of phrasing. It made me think, however, that it was also deep and maybe theological.

Ashlin has the faith of a child. The things she is thankful for are truly, in her mind, thank-yous to God.

It reminded me of the book of James, where Jesus' brother wrote, "Every good and perfect gift is from above, coming down from the Father of the heavenly lights." Paul also encouraged us to present our requests to God "with thanksgiving" (Philippians 4:6).

Maybe there's a subtle difference between *thankful* and *thanksgiving*. Perhaps the former is more about *my* emotion and experience of gratitude than the latter, which is directed toward the one responsible for our blessing.

Maybe there's a difference in our hearts between *thankful* and *thank you*.

Whether there's a deep theological distinction here or not, that night my little angel brought tears to my eyes and taught her dad about purity of heart and what it looks like to truly be *thank you* to God.

WHERE WE'RE HEADED

Life finds its harmony when we're centered on God, walking in faith, and experiencing the fullness of life He designed for us to experience.

From here we'll begin examining what the Bible and some of the great Christian thinkers have to say about faith, and what that means in light of preconceived ideas about Christianity and given our place in the context of contemporary culture. In doing so, we will answer some of Christians' most heartfelt questions:

- Do we have the wrong definition of faith? (chap. 3)
- How do I talk to God? More important, how do I hear from God? (chap. 4)
- What is God up to in this world? (chap. 5)
- Do I have to give up the things that make me happy to have faith? (chap. 6)
- I have doubts . . . does that mean I don't have faith? (chap. 7)
- What is God calling me, personally, to do? (chaps. 8 and 9)
- This world is crazy . . . how am I supposed to live for God? (chaps. 10 and 11)

- Do we really need church? (chap. 12)
- What is it all for? (chaps. 13, 14, 15)

But first we need to look at how irrational and upside down walking by faith can truly seem.

PARADOX

Such welcome and unwelcome things at once
'Tis hard to reconcile.[1]
—William Shakespeare

In the 1500s, there lived a wealthy statesman named Michel de Montaigne. Over a short period of time, he lost his best friend and five of his six children. In 1571, he retired from public life and, during a reclusion that lasted nearly ten years, he explored and wrote about the most troubling aspects of human experience and existence. He called these short writings *essays* (French for "trial" or "attempt"), thereby inventing the modern writing form "essay."

In his writings, Montaigne revived a form of skepticism from Ancient Greece that posited the apparent contradictions and inscrutability of life's great questions. A more recent book by Sarah Bakewell—*How to Live: Or, A Life of Montaigne in One Question and Twenty Attempts at an Answer*—resurrects Montaigne's insights.[2] One age-old central question—"How should we live?"—and twenty attempts at an answer amid the messiness of life . . . all in one amusingly honest title.

Montaigne was one among many of the great thinkers and writers in history who discovered that life is fraught with paradox. And so is faith.

FAITH AS PARADOX

A *paradox* is an apparent contradiction, a statement about reality that seems antithetical. Some paradoxes are common and well understood. We all know what it means to speak of a memory or a victory or a relationship as "bittersweet." And most entrepreneurs understand that "to make money, you have to spend money."

Between ages three and six, I lived in Holland. For me, the memories of that time and place are just like the movie portrayals of the Netherlands—windmills, tulips, and frozen dikes and canals on which to skate during long, cold winters. We even had a small pond some hundred feet from our back door that froze every winter.

Because I was so young, my mom was careful to communicate time and again the danger of falling through thin ice while skating. She repeatedly taught me that if I ever fell through the ice, I should swim for the dark—not the light—spot above me. This is certainly counterintuitive, but the ice itself looks white from underneath, while the hole in the ice—the path of salvation—appears dark.

Walking by faith rather than sight requires awareness that our eyes can play tricks, reality can be deceiving, and the true path is often counterintuitive.

Life isn't always logically grounded. Often, we're hopelessly lost in the nuance and uncertainty of life. The result is, we're all hungry for concrete answers to deep questions: *Why am I here? What is God's will for my life?* And as we discussed in the last chapter, *how do I really follow God in areas where it feels absurd?*

SCRIPTURE DOESN'T HELP

The paradoxical nature of reality is reflected in Scripture. God's Word doesn't sweep the confusing nature of life under the rug, but instead frames the paradox even more explicitly.

Consider these two verses from Luke:

"Glory to God in the highest heaven,
     and on earth peace to those on whom his favor rests." (2:14)

"Do you think I came to bring peace on earth? No, I tell you, but division." (12:51)

This bizarre contradiction is between two verses *in the same book*. Jesus says something even more inflammatory later, in Luke 14:26: "If anyone comes to me and does not hate father and mother, wife and children, brothers and sisters—yes, even their own life—such a person cannot be my disciple." Why is one of the Ten Commandments to honor your parents if Jesus says to hate them?

Logic might lead us to simply dismiss Jesus at this point, but look at what He did in His final moments, while hanging on the cross: "When Jesus saw his mother there, and the disciple whom he loved standing nearby, he said to her, 'Woman, here is your son,' and to the disciple, 'Here is your mother.' From that time on, this disciple took her into his home" (John 19:26–27). If Jesus wants everyone to hate his or her mother, why did He take such loving care of His own mother?

Paul asserted in Ephesians 2:8–9 that we are saved by faith, not by works. Yet James said to a different church that without works, faith is worthless (2:26).

God asks us to draw near to Him and promises He will draw near to us (cf. James 4:8), yet the Psalms often lament the hiddenness of God (cf. Psalm 22:1–3).

What's going on? Are these passages in conflict, or are they paradoxically pointing out different aspects of faith and obedience?

Think back to the account of Jericho. From our perspective, in hindsight, it all seems to come together and make sense. We understand the value of a memorial, and we know the time spent building one at the Jordan crossing didn't end up costing a victory or exposing the people to an enemy attack. The Israelites won the victory over a walled city with no loss of life among them. God received the glory, and His people learned (again) not to put their trust in human leaders or their schemes, but instead to obey the will of the One who alone delivers.

But what if we were there without the benefit of hindsight? Would human logic tell us something different? When entering enemy territory, soldiers ought to be in the lead, not priests. Taking the time to lift heavy rocks out of the streambed, commemorating an event when the outcome is still very much in doubt, is just foolishness. It is the strength of armies and weapons that win battles against fortified cities, not the noise of shouting and trumpets. Spoils go to the victors, not to a spirit-deity who has no use for them.

From the perspective of the Israelites themselves, every aspect of God's command was—at that time—counterintuitive and paradoxical.

POETIC PARADOX

Why is walking by faith better than walking by sight? Because sight alone will not convince us that living for others and trusting God's leading will lead to life. Early on, our church adopted the motto, coined by our former college pastor Matt Smith: "Give your life away." The foundation of our local church rests on the idea that we will only find life by losing it. Scripture and Christian faith are replete with many other life-giving paradoxes:

- Die to live.
- Serve to gain.
- Give to receive.

- Lose your life to find it.
- The first will be last.
- The weak will be strong.
- Walk by faith, not by sight.
- Suffering can be blessing.

LIVING THE QUESTION

While in seminary, I ran across the author Henri Nouwen, who articulated the tension—or paradox—of faith as well as anyone I have read. His answer, unlike most I have heard, does not whitewash the messiness of life or explain away the mystery of God. Rather, Nouwen wrote that an essential part of life is learning to "live the questions" faith engenders.[3]

To wait on the Lord.

To pray our pain.

To accept confusion.

Nouwen's answer resonates with the honest picture of faith I see in Scripture. Life is, as stated by my Old Testament professor, *relentlessly difficult*. Jesus promised suffering in Matthew 16:24, and as testified in Scripture, those most clearly called by God and most definitively used by God often are given the most challenging circumstances.

Life is messy. God is mysterious. And accepting this tension-filled truth, no matter the circumstances, is the pathway to peace.

LOST IN THE CLOUDS

My dad was an exchange pilot with the Dutch Navy flying the P-3 Orion back when we lived in Holland. He was forced to rely on instruments many times in order to get back to his base. On one occasion, he was returning from a long ocean surveillance mission to an airfield at Land's End in England, where the weather had deteriorated into heavy fog.

With less than an eighth of a mile of visibility, he had to make several landing attempts until finally the copilot saw the runway lights emerge at only a hundred feet above the ground. When they finally landed, the fog was so thick that my dad couldn't see where he was or where to turn. The tower helped them by sending a "follow-me" truck to guide the airplane to the ramp.

When my dad told me his zero visibility stories, he explained how, without sight, one's equilibrium can be thrown off. Vertigo, he told me, is thinking you are turning when you are actually level, or thinking you are actually level when you are turning. Because you can't see, your inner ear begins sending your brain false signals. When experiencing vertigo a pilot must be disciplined and rely on his or her instruments, otherwise they might steer the aircraft into the ground while mistakenly believing they are flying straight and level.

Sooner or later, Dad said, a pilot will find himself in a cloud, or fog, or haze and will have to rely solely on instruments. The instrument panel provides an artificial horizon that pilots must *trust* regardless of what their senses are telling them. It requires training to develop the confidence to overcome our natural instincts and *trust* what the instruments are saying.

Zero visibility landings can only be accomplished when you have total faith and trust in what your instruments are telling you, even when your senses contradict what you see plainly before you.

The paradoxical nature of the Christian life can give us an awkward sense of not knowing up from down. But I have learned that God's commands, our trust in His promises, and our reliance on His guidance are the instruments by which we fly.

The temptation when we're living in the midst of the paradox is to pull back, recoil, lean more on our own understanding, and resist entering into God's plan for us. In times of uncertainty, we can begin to steer ourselves away from God and toward our own sense of reason. But Proverbs 3:5–7 says:

Trust in the Lord with all your heart
 and lean not on your own understanding;
in all your ways submit to him,
 and he will make your paths straight.
Do not be wise in your own eyes;
 fear the Lord and shun evil.

  The secret to understanding where to go in life is found not in navigating our way to safety, but rather simply trusting in God's leading. Trusting that He is good. Trusting that even if we don't like where He takes us, He's taking us there for a reason.

CATCH-22

The idea of the *catch-22* came into our collective vocabulary from the Joseph Heller novel of the same name. The story involved a fictional World War II air force squadron. The rigors of air combat—the continual need to kill or be killed—could drive a pilot crazy. Recognizing this hazard and not wanting its ranks filled with crazy airmen, the air force instituted a voluntary process for identifying such men. Pilots in the squadron were given the option of taking a psychological evaluation; if they were declared insane, they would be released from further combat.

  But there was a catch, referred to in the relevant manual as "Catch-22." Requesting a psychological evaluation was deemed proof of an airman's sanity, since it would be crazy not to seek a release from further combat duty.

  A catch-22 is not a paradox. Instead, it is a hopeless trap of frustrating, inescapable circularity.

  Our tendency is to think that the paradox of faith is a catch-22: if I act selfishly, I'll be unhappy, but if I act selflessly, I'll lose all the things that make me happy. But the catch-22 isn't the whole story: the contradiction is broken by the presence of God.

Walking by sight doesn't bring the control or sense of satisfaction we desire, and, over time, it guarantees a measure of suffering. Walking by faith, on the other hand, can feel like walking blind—an even more dangerous idea—and we know that it, too, will involve suffering. Both alternatives seem undesirable.

It is the faithfulness, the promise, and the presence of God that give us a way out of the catch-22. He promises a path of life *through* the paradox:

- Whoever finds their life will lose it, and whoever loses their life for my sake *will find it* (Matthew 10:39).
- It is *more blessed* to give than to receive (Acts 20:35).
- *Givers prosper*; misers lose everything (Proverbs 11:24).
- *Blessed are* the poor in spirit (Matthew 5:3).
- Refresh others and *you will be refreshed* (Proverbs 11:25).

Walking in the paradox is only possible if God's view is bigger than the human view. We have a limited view of reality. God, we're told, has an all-knowing perspective.

Even so, the questions are relentless: Is this all just a bunch of Christian spiritual talk? Should I really risk everything and bank on God? How do I know that God will catch me if I take the leap off the cliff?

Faith is the art of living forward in obedience, not in the absence of questions like these, but in the face of them.

Faith marches through the paradox.

Trust in the LORD with all your heart and lean not on
your own understanding; in all your ways submit to
him, and he will make your paths straight.
—PROVERBS 3:5–6

WHAT KIERKEGAARD KNEW

If anyone thinks he is Christian and yet is indifferent towards
his being a Christian, then he really is not one at all. What
would we think of a man who affirmed that he was in love
and also that it was a matter of indifference to him?[1]
—SØREN KIERKEGAARD

When I was in high school, there were a lot of Christians of one kind
or another. The funny thing was, nobody really acted like a Christian.
Christian faith, at bottom, meant simply belief that God exists and a loose
identification with the Christian religion, with maybe a few theological
details or ideas about the Bible thrown in. It didn't really have much to do
with how you lived or made decisions.

Our modern American definition of the word *faith* can be anemic and
hollow. We think believing God exists is the end of the story, never considering that God might desire more of us than simply acknowledging He is there.

This is true now, and it was true in Jesus' time. In the apostle James's
passage on faith, he surfaced this kind of thin faith by saying, "You believe

that there is one God. Good!" He then pointed out the irony by sarcastically adding, "Even the demons believe that" (2:19).

If "believing in God" isn't all that is meant by faith, what is faith? Could God be calling us to something more than we have been taught to think?

This anemic definition of Christian faith was also prevalent in the nineteenth-century Danish church, during the life of one of Christianity's most provocative pens: Søren Kierkegaard. He spent his life conducting what he called an "attack on Christendom," trying to return the church to a robust, true definition of faith.

I remember being twenty-six, reclining on a lumpy futon, with warm sunlight streaming in through the window of my rented room in La Mirada, California. I was flipping through the pages of Kierkegaard's book *Fear and Trembling*, hungry for clarity. Fresh out of a relationship, I was wrestling with God over the pressing question of marriage.

I was dying to know whether or not I'd ever be married. All I wanted was a straight answer. If the answer was no, then I'd drop the issue, move on, and never worry about it again. But if I was going to get married, I wanted to know when. At least then I could remove myself from the emotional frenzy of dating, put my head down, and continue working hard.

But I learned something during that season of wrestling with God: in the midst of uncertainties about life and the big picture, real faith doesn't allow for easy answers.

Kierkegaard's insight in *Fear and Trembling* began to unlock for me the mystery of trusting God. He taught me that, like so many other aspects of the Christian life, faith demands the ability to remain caught in the balance. Living the question. Suspended in tension.

KIERKEGAARD, MAGNETS, AND UNGROUNDED FAITH

Fear and Trembling is Kierkegaard's philosophical interpretation of the story of Abraham and Isaac in Genesis 22:1–19, which he published under a pseudonym, Johannes de Silencio. In this book, Kierkegaard deepens the definition of faith by pointing out two elements of the story that we shouldn't miss: (1) faith can be perplexing, unreasonable, and scary; and (2) faith requires a blind leap to trust.

The story begins before Isaac was born. God promised that Abraham would be the father of a large nation, even though he and his wife were barren and she was past childbearing age. Finally, after decades of waiting, Isaac, the promised miracle child, was born.

But several years later, God gave Abraham an incomprehensible command: "Go to Mount Moriah and sacrifice your son." Abraham left the next morning, made the journey, climbed the mountain with Isaac, and prepared to sacrifice his beloved son. But just before he killed Isaac, God stopped him and instructed him to sacrifice a ram caught in the bushes instead.

Picture the story: Abraham gets up the morning of the sacrifice and says nothing to anyone, not even his wife. There's really nothing he can say, right? What God is asking him to do is so outside the bounds of reason, wisdom, and ethics that he can't tell anybody about it. It is the ideal example of unreasonable faith.

There's no morality or logic Abraham can lean on to defend or explain to his wife or others what he's about to do. God is calling him to do something in faith that is completely unreasonable. I like to say it this way: true faith is "ungrounded"—the resolution isn't always apparent.

Imagine trying to fly a magnet through the center of a metal pipe without letting it touch the sides. There is constant energy pulling the magnet toward one side or the other, to ground it on the side of the pipe. Keeping the magnet in the center requires a lot of tension, energy, and effort. But if it slips just a little in one direction, it grounds on the pipe's wall, and suddenly the tension and difficulty are over.

That's how Abraham must have felt: caught in the middle, completely in tension between what he knew God had asked of him and what he must have wanted to do. The sides of the pipe represent all the things that make it easier to trust God: certainty, foreknowledge, satisfaction, and reason. But when we act on faith, we remain trembling in the center, unable to touch the sides.

Faith often feels that way. This is not a chapter about sacrificing sons or selling everything you own. It is a chapter about God's call and our response. It is about our willingness to live by genuine faith.

The problem is we are always trying to walk by sight but call it faith.

If God calls us to something extreme or absurd (Kierkegaard's favorite word for faith), we can feel a little bit like the magnet flying through the metal pipe. We're trying desperately to move forward, but at every moment we want to veer off and ground our faith somehow—like the magnet continuously being drawn to the sides of the metal pipe. We look for something that will relieve the uncertainty and give us a sense of why God is calling us in that direction or how everything will turn out. We look for certainty. We hunger for closure.

Every Christian has wrestled with this at some level. We seek to resolve tensions as fast as we can.

Obedience is frequently the opposite. It is a jump into the unknown. A move based on trust, not in a certain future, but in a dependable God.

If you are called to leave a steady job, trusting that God will provide, you are living this out. If you leave a peer group, believing God is calling you elsewhere, you experience the anxiety of faith. If you move to a country that lacks law and order to work for justice, you're giving away your protection, yet trusting that God will somehow take care of you.

Today, as when Jesus lived, there are very few people who are willing to treat the weightier matters of life with absolute surrender.

We want to call ourselves Christians, but are we willing to go beyond only believing God is there and actually trust and follow Him? As the Abraham story illustrates, the stakes are high.

GROUNDING OUR FAITH

Kierkegaard used the Abraham story to talk about the ways we escape faith by grounding our trust in something other than faith, something more stable and controllable—and ultimately meaningless.

The natural thing to do when we're feeling like the magnet flying through the pipe is to find ways to ground ourselves. When we are plagued by anxiety, stress, or uncertainty, we naturally try to find relief. When God calls us to do something scary or difficult, we usually want some kind of guarantee or security blanket to make the task seem safer and easier. The most common ways we do this are by resigning ourselves to our fates, by playing the martyr, by drowning God out with other voices, or by using our imaginations. Let's take a look at each of these.

RESIGNATION

Kierkegaard allegorized his greatest weakness in faith with the "knight of resignation." The knight of resignation grounds emotion by dutifully resigning or giving in to God's control. The person who turns to resignation will say things like "I guess that's just God's will"; "I guess God wants me to suffer"; or, "I guess that's what I get for wanting my own way."

Resignation can give us a sense of independence. It is different from submitting humbly and joyfully to the call of Christ. When I resign myself to God's control, God has my feet but not my heart. He has my movement, but not my trust. Much like a prisoner being dragged along in handcuffs behind a jailer, we are walking the same direction He is, but we're not really following or trusting in His goodness. *Resignation, a finish line of sorts, is the reward.*

Resignation is synonymous with suppressing desire in an attempt to be more spiritual. But we see that Jesus' desires were very much at work in his faith: "Jesus . . . *for the joy that was set before him* endured the cross, despising the shame, and is seated at the right hand of the throne of God" (Hebrews 12:2 ESV; emphasis added).

When we turn to resignation to ground our emotions, we forget or ignore God's promise and lose sight of His goodness. It's not that we have to believe everything will turn out good in the end, but assuming it won't or assuming God doesn't care isn't trusting in His goodness.

Resigning is not following—it's finalizing. Resignation quits; faith hopes.

MARTYRDOM

Martyr complexes are another way we ground our faith. "God has decided to bless me with this horrible burden, just like He always does. I guess it's because He knows I can handle it and will always follow Him." Martyrs seek to find satisfaction in being the person who is suffering or struggling. *The reputation is the reward.*

The martyr complex is an easy trap for leaders to fall into. It was this very thing that led Moses to strike the rock instead of speaking to it, as God instructed him in Numbers 20:8. His sister had just died, there was no water, and his people complained and panicked for what probably seemed like the hundredth time. God told him to speak to a rock, and water would flow out of it.

In a fit of emotion and frustration, Moses played the martyr. He called the Israelites "rebels" and struck the rock with his staff instead of speaking to it. Though God chose to provide water anyway, He was so angry that He forbade Moses to ever enter the promised land. God cares a great deal about faithful obedience, the kind of obedience grounded only in faith and hope, without our added ways of resolving the felt tension.

OTHER VOICES

Some of us choose to drown out God's voice with other voices. We read an endless stack of Christian books, seek advice from family and friends, and look for anything we can to provide some logical reasons why we shouldn't do what God is asking us to do. We start looking for safer, less absurd, and more seemingly spiritual options and rationale. *Bathing in spiritual conversation, as a way of ignoring or minimizing the tension of God's call, is the reward.*

That's what King Saul was after when he went to see a medium in 1 Samuel 28. God wasn't telling him what he wanted to hear, so he decided to find his own answers by contacting his dead mentor. We do the same thing when we look for reasonable alternatives to God's will that fit more comfortably into our lives.

There is much wisdom in listening to your spouse, reading Christian books, and seeking advice. But we run into problems when we use those things to deliberately drown out God's calling or direction, when we busy ourselves with what looks to be wise in an effort to avoid heeding God's call.

IMAGINATION

The way I sometimes attempt to ground my faith is by using my imagination. Instead of allowing trust to drive my obedience, I let my imagination fill in the reasons why God is asking me to do something. "Of course, God. By letting go of this opportunity now, I'm freeing my hands to receive this other one. I see how this will play out." By exploring all the wonderful reasons why God might be asking me to trust Him, I reason myself into surrender. *Imagination dreams up a potential reward.*

But, again, creative intellect is not faith. On my best days, it is part of my hope and belief in God's goodness. On my worst days, it is less about faith and more about fantasy.

My dreams may or may not have truth in them. Regardless, it is God I should follow in faith, not my imagination.

TRUST + OBEDIENCE = FAITH

All four perspectives lose sight of the fact that God isn't cruel. He doesn't require us to surrender what we love most because He delights in taking away our joy (a severely misaligned perspective I have encountered in a lot of believers). God requires surrender because that is the only way we can truly find Him. It is only there that trust is made real.

All of the Beatitudes express this to some degree. We don't typically think that the meek are the ones who are going to be glorified. Or that the persecuted are going to be blessed. Or that the peacemakers are going to somehow get ahead in life. Yet in Jesus' formula, and in the upside-down logic of His kingdom, becoming weak in the eyes of the world ultimately leads to our greatest blessing and fuels the happiness that we all crave.

When we look at God's covenant with Abraham, we see that because Abraham *obeyed*, God said He would keep His promise (Genesis 22:16–18).

This is the first time in the Old Testament that a form of the word *obedience* is used. That seems significant to me. Abraham's story, the biblical picture of faith, the story of the man whose faith was credited to him as righteousness, is the first story where God uses the word *obey*.

However, there is something we can't overlook if we are trying to understand what faith actually is. God praised Abraham's obedience. But notice that Abraham never actually *carried out* the sacrifice. So how did God know Abraham had obeyed? Kierkegaard points out that Abraham *made the decision* to obey, and moved forward *with certainty that God would deliver* on His promise. But he was stopped before the deed was done.

The point? Faith is not mere resignation to obedience, simply *doing* what God asks. It doesn't believe that God has destined us to suffer. It does not covet wisdom from others or worship intellect. Faithful obedience is inseparable from the *belief* in God's trustworthiness that subsequently moves us to follow, trust, and obey Him. Faith is unconditionally trusting God and acting as He commands.

THE LEAP OF FAITH

Kierkegaard surfaces the tension: true faith is more than just giving up. It is more than feeling cursed and accepting a gloomy outlook on life. Faith is more than public opinion or punishing oneself.

True faith is a radical obedience, a willingness to risk everything—surrender anything—with the belief God can, and will, reward the faithful and make firm our hopes.

This is why Jesus speaks of faith as small as a mustard seed. The idea isn't the size of faith. What matters is simply the presence of true faith—the willingness, in fear and trembling, of the one with barely a shred of faith to walk forward in obedience and hope.

One of the scariest and most confusing elements of Abraham's story is that he was asked to sacrifice the very thing God had promised him—his son. To have faith, he had to believe that God would keep His promise, *and* he had to obey by destroying that promise. To have faith, we have to be willing to give up the promise itself—to hold the blessings of God more loosely than God Himself.

Kierkegaard doesn't offer us much comfort: "No, the easiness of Christianity is distinguished by one thing only: by the difficulty. Thus its yoke is easy and its burden light—for the person who has cast off all his burdens, all of them, the burdens of hope and of fear and of despondency and of despair—but it is very difficult."[2]

The prize is inextricable from the sacrifice.

Faith offers God the very best of what we have. Trust puts its greatest security on the line and says, "Nothing will I hold back from You, Lord." The comfort and the promise of faith is that God will deliver, make good on His covenant, and lead us where He knows we are meant to go. When we have faith, God proves faithful. When we trust, God proves trustworthy.

In one of his other works, Kierkegaard coined the phrase "a leap of faith," which has often been wrongly assumed to mean that belief in God is irrational. However, Kierkegaard's point has much more to do with obedience to God when you don't have rational reasons or information to motivate the action—nothing except a trust in the faithfulness of God.

When we take the leap of faith, we are always going to be living out a kind of anxiety, emotion, and fear . . . in spite of these emotions we trust that God is going to keep the promises He has made.

The leap of faith isn't always extreme, and it doesn't always look the way we think it will. Americans often have a "bigger is better" mind-set. But it's not about the size of the leap; it's about the leap itself.

Maybe it would be more accurate if we used the phrase "leap *to* faith."

I have several friends who have passed up lucrative careers to continue doing difficult, unflattering, often dangerous justice work. Their obedience to what God wants them to do has been lived out daily for years and even decades.

Throughout the history of Antioch Church in Bend, Oregon, where I pastor, and in the programs that have found their beginnings within our church family (the internship for college students and graduates, and Kilns

College, the school of theology and justice), I have seen expressions of the kind of faith that Kierkegaard means. Time and again I have watched as different people move forward to join in what God is doing because they've sensed Him calling them here. From one of the first staff members, who moved here to serve the church voluntarily while working at Starbucks to make ends meet, to the interns and Kilns students who have given up their security and future plans, I have seen many take the step forward in faith for the sake of heeding God's call. In many cases, their decisions haven't been the safest decisions, nor did they come with a guaranteed end result.

The point is that they each have been assured that they were being called, but unsure of what it was they were being drawn into. Still, they went. This is what a friend of mine calls "necessary endings," moments when you realize the time has come for the current season to end and a new one to begin. You may not know where you're going, but you know you need to go.

Starting a family seems to happen this way. When you are sure of the fact that you want to marry the person you love, or when you and your spouse know that it's the time for kids, you don't wait until you have the money (you'll never reach the point where you think you have enough); you just do it.

Being generous with money and tithing are similar moments of faith. They are moments that come as a regular reminder of the fact that handing over our money and trusting God with our finances just doesn't make sense. But God gives us the grace; we do it anyway; and we are able to catch a greater glimpse of His faithfulness because of it.

What Kierkegaard knew is this: we are required to step out in authentic faith, not in resignation or creative imagination. In the midst of uncertainty and the paradoxical tension of having to believe God for the impossible, real faith requires actually trusting in *Him*, despite our inability to always understand Him.

The leap of faith is all about the moment of trust, not the size of the jump. Imagine you're standing in a thick fog, and you can't see more than a few inches in front of you. You don't know what hazards or cliffs may be around you. But God has told you to walk. The leap of faith is simply the move forward.

Even an inch or two is a leap forward into faith.

God may call us to move an inch or a mile. We might find resolution in a second or grope our way through the fog of faith for a decade. We won't know before we leap . . . but we do know this: taking Kierkegaard's leap is the answer to the paradox of the messiness of life, the mystery of God, and the challenge of authentic spirituality.

Whether faith feels like a big leap; a long, slow journey; or a combination of both, it involves obedience. As mentioned previously, faith is not simply believing God exists or having a thin feeling that He is good. Faith, true Abrahamic faith, takes the shape of obedience.

But in order to obey, we need to know what God wants us to do.

The Bible gives us the big picture of God's character and how He wants us to live. But wouldn't it be nice if we could get our hands on what He specifically wants us to do? Wouldn't it be ideal if we could engage with God in our own specific contexts? What if we could feel that we know God, could hear His voice, and know what He's asking?

We can, and that's where prayer enters the equation. The question we turn to next is: How can we hear God?

To the faithful you show yourself faithful.
—Psalm 18:25

WISDOM'S FOLLY

There is not in the world a kind of life more sweet and
delightful than that of a continual conversation with God.[1]
—BROTHER LAWRENCE

My journey toward learning more about prayer really began with my disillusionment with it. Fresh out of a fraternity at Clemson University and new
to the Christian scene, I often found myself annoyed by Christian behaviors.

The way people prayed in groups always had a strange, inauthentic
feeling. For example, leaders would say, "Pray for the person on your left,"
or, "Pray for the person across from you." And when prayer requests were
taken, they began to sound like an infirmary report: "God, please heal my
cold. Lord, please help Aunt Mildred's big toe."

Then there was the felt performance or audition aspect to prayer. This
was exemplified during and after one of the first times I prayed aloud in a
group setting (among the full staff at a Christian camp). As I prayed, there
were all sorts of "Mmms," "ahs," and "amens." Afterward, the camp cook
put her arms around me and said, "What a beautiful prayer." The old janitor

said, "That was powerful and deep," and there was more of the like. Their comments were well-intentioned, but had the effect of tuning my thoughts more to the affirmation of friends than to the conversation with Christ.

There was also the problem of my attention span. It took me years to find out that I'm not the only person who falls asleep during other people's lengthy, verbose prayers, or who begins to think about football or movies.

My mind also wandered to analyzing people's motives, as it often seemed as if there was an ulterior motive behind the prayer or that it was being used as a tool to get the attention of someone else in the room (which seemed to happen a lot when it was single guys who were praying).

I thought these were normal prayer experiences, what Christians—and the Bible—meant by "prayer." I hadn't yet learned that prayer could actually mean the powerful thing that happened when I was alone with God.

My first year as a Christian was a particularly difficult one, as I lost most of my friends at the university because of my newly professed commitment to follow Jesus. I would be in my dorm room at the fraternity hall late into the night, waiting for the noise of guys coming home from the bars at 2 a.m.— there was no point in going to sleep any earlier. In that solitary space, filled with many questions and much confusion, I read, talked to God, searched the Scriptures, wrote in a journal, and went to sleep picturing myself being close to the One who refers to Himself as a rock and a strong tower.

In private, my communication with God grew to be very conversational and intimate. God sustained me in times of struggle, and reminded me of things I needed to know in times of challenge. All of this was very different from what went on in public and from what I had thought was meant by prayer.

The experience that collapsed the divide between public and private prayer occurred when I was sitting at an In-N-Out Burger in Southern California in the spring of 1999. I had started eating my usual Double-Double when out of the corner of my eye I spotted some folks from church at another table. Quickly, I bowed my head and assumed the prescribed posture for praying over my meal, not wanting these other Christians to think I had neglected the ritual.

Immediately the hypocrisy hit me. At home alone, I had no difficulty talking to God before, during, and after a meal, with little regard for what anyone else thought. But simply because of the presence of other Christians in a public setting, all of a sudden I was contorting my body to look like I was praying.

A passage from the Gospels came to mind, in which Jesus said that when we pray we're supposed to go into a closet so as not to be seen by men. We're not to be like the religious leaders who prayed publicly and ceremonially with the desire to be noticed (receiving accolades from the janitor or hugs from the camp cook).[2]

I decided right then and there to take a break—what I called a prayer fast—from all public prayer. In group settings, I refrained from praying, instead reading from the Psalms. When the staff at the church where I worked would gather for staff prayer, I'd go find a hidden corner in my office and spend the time fully alone with God, saying nothing to be heard by human ears and doing my best to listen for the rhythm of the conversation that God wanted to have.

I began to drive to places in Los Angeles to spend the day in solitude, trying to allow my prayer life to reflect the nature of the prayer life Jesus exemplified with His Father. At first I'd only be able to take the quiet and solitude for an hour or so before my mind would whirl with other things and the stresses of the day. But before long I would spend the better part of the day at the Huntington Library in Pasadena, stilling my heart before God and learning to tune my ear to His voice.

Eventually, spending time during the day once or twice a week wasn't enough, and I began getting in my car late at night to drive the Southern California freeways with my window down and sunroof open, with no destination in mind and no other purpose than spending that time alone with God.

I believe I experienced something like what Paul envisioned when he told the young believers at Thessalonica to "pray without ceasing," or when he wrote of the "fellowship of the Holy Spirit."[3]

In my experience, public prayer is fraught with potential problems that obscure the conversational nature of true prayer. Of course, public

31

corporate prayer does have a place. Acts 12:5 describes how the believers in Jerusalem gathered together to pray earnestly for Peter when he was in prison (and later verses describe how God answered those prayers). There are many other instances like this described in the New Testament. But the nature of such corporate prayer is often starkly different from our modern version of it.

The early church sometimes expressed their prayers in a song; at other times, the whole congregation beseeched God while flat on their faces in repentance or anguish. These and other New Testament examples seem in stark contrast to finding myself in a plush living room praying for the person on my left or for the greater comfort of the privileged 1 percent of humanity living in the developed world.

True prayer—whether done publicly or privately—is about conversing with and paying attention to God from a posture of humility and with a willingness to listen. There is a natural rhythm to prayer reflected in the Psalms. The psalmist intimately cried out to God about the broad state of his emotions, almost always with a remembrance of God's great works and faithfulness in the past and from a position of confidence in His great works and faithfulness to come.

The Bible certainly encourages sharing our concerns with our Maker; Paul told the Philippians, "Present your requests to God," and Jesus commended persistence in His parable of the widow before the judge.[4] But Scripture knows nothing of long, endless lists of wants, wishes, and needs put before God as if He were a Santa Claus who is open for business all year.

Jesus admonished that "when you pray, do not keep on babbling like pagans, for they think they will be heard because of their many words. Do not be like them, for your Father knows what you need before you ask him."[5] When I come to God in prayer, I have to remind myself that He knows me better than I know Him, that He understands my emotional state better than I do.

When I only *think* I know what is best, He *knows* what is best and how to lead me to it.

PRIVILEGE AND HUMILITY

Gratitude and humility are largely absent from a lot of prayer displayed in much of the church today. The great privilege of having direct access to God in prayer was bought for us at a very great price—the excruciating and humiliating death of Jesus on a Roman cross.

Before that event, access to God was extremely limited. For God's own people, direct contact with God was mediated through a high priest, who could only come before him in the holiest place of the temple once a year. And while we find the prayers of the prophets and psalmists recorded in the Old Testament, for the most part it was God who initiated communication (as with Abraham, Moses, the prophets, and the judges).

Are we sufficiently appreciative of this? As the writer of Hebrews wrote, we can come boldly before the throne of God, and as Jesus prayed, we can cry out to God as our "Abba" (Father), a term of familiarity and intimacy.[6]

As followers of Christ, we do well to acknowledge that in Him we are adopted as sons and daughters, and Jesus calls us "friends."[7]

And yet, do we appropriate this wonderful privileged status with a proper sense of awe, worship, and humility? When God spoke to Moses, he took off his sandals and hid his face in fear; Isaiah declared himself "undone" and "unclean" in the face of God's holiness.[8]

As we enter into the presence of God as adopted sons and daughters, by His grace and through His encouragement, our boldness should be tempered with humility, and we should never forget the holiness and power of the One with whom we are communicating.

HEARING GOD

The paradox of faith is answered in our willingness to walk into our greatest fears and uncertainties with confidence in Christ. Conversational prayer that orients us to God—rather than prayer that tries to get God to orient Himself to us—informs our faith and makes it possible. To put it another way, our ability to embrace a life of bold and dynamic faith is closely tied to having confidence in what God is telling us.

One follower of Christ who did this very successfully was Brother Lawrence (1611–1691), who, as a kitchen worker in a Carmelite lay community, became widely known for his perpetual intimacy with God. His own account of this intimacy—written in Medieval French and translated into English as *The Practice of the Presence of God*—has been, for generations, one of the classic Christian treatises on the devotional life.

Asked by others how they could experience this same intimacy with God, Brother Lawrence replied:

> Stop putting your trust in human rules, devotional exercises and acts of penance. Instead, exercise a living, obedient faith in God. Live as though he were beside you and with you all the time—*as indeed he is.* Seek to do what he wants, as and when he commands it, and make his command your joy and chief pleasure. The man who lives like that will be fully human, completely Christian and genuinely happy.[9]

When understood this way, what's really at issue here is not limited to our prayer life but extends to our entire mental life. Think about it: God has just as much access to all our other thoughts as He does to those specifically directed to Him in the form of prayers.

So, the questions naturally surface, "How do I hear God? How do we know when He speaks?"

The answer has several facets. Though there is no magic formula (contrary to the prevailing pop-Christian message), there are certainly things that help set us up for better hearing the voice of God as He is leading us.

SETTING THE STAGE

A true prerequisite to hearing God's voice is obedience.

Matthew 5:8 says, "Blessed are the pure in heart, for they will see God." Similarly, Psalm 24:3–4 says:

34

> Who may ascend the mountain of the LORD?
> Who may stand in his holy place?
> The one who has clean hands and a pure heart,
> who does not trust in an idol
> or swear by a false god.

Sin disrupts our relationship with God. As an affair damages the relationship with a spouse and robs it of the joy that could be, sin causes a breach in our relationship with God that robs us of the joy that He wants us to have in community with Him. This naturally has an impact on our ability to hear and understand God.

Proverbs 15:29 says, "The LORD is far from the wicked, but he hears the prayer of the righteous." It stands to reason that if we find ourselves out of step with God, we must repent. We must come back into alignment with God by accepting responsibility for the breach in relationship and turning back to Him in purity of heart.

Practically, it is when we are in right relationship with God that we hear Him best.

WHERE IS GOD ALREADY SPEAKING?

God is already speaking in certain areas, and as Elijah learned, God is often in the still, small voice and not always in the thunder.[10] Where do we go to hear that clear but quiet voice?

First, God speaks in nature. Psalm 19:1 tells us, "The heavens declare the glory of God; the skies proclaim the work of his hands." When we are out in God's creation, we open ourselves to an awareness of His power, His glory, His faithfulness, and His love. When we remove ourselves from the noise and clutter of our urban settings, our offices, and our devices, we carve out the space and solitude to meet God in the place He created and called "good" (see Genesis 1). Incidentally, we are thereby aligning ourselves with God's people throughout the ages, for whom creation served as the holy place where they found God and where He spoke to them.

Second, God clearly speaks in Scripture. Psalm 119:9–10 says, "How can a young man keep his way pure? By living according to your word. I seek you with all my heart." Hebrews 4:12 teaches us that "the word of God is alive and active. Sharper than any double-edged sword, it penetrates even to dividing soul and spirit, joints and marrow; it judges the thoughts and attitudes of the heart."

Through reading and diligent study of the Bible, we find that God makes Himself, His ways, and His thoughts known to us. His Spirit inside us has a miraculous way of tying the propositional truths of His revelation in Scripture to our lives and helping us know how to act and respond in the various situations we face.

What if we so immersed ourselves in knowledge of God's Word that we saw the world and all it contains through a biblical lens? Our interaction with Scripture ought to be the main thing that colors and shapes all of our paradigms.

One day I had to get all the tires on both our cars replaced because someone had come through our neighborhood and slashed them—all eight. I spent the entire day with a guy from our local tire store, and he knew everything you could want to know about tires.

As Chet was shuttling me back to my house and cars were passing by, I asked if all he sees are tires. He said that he did indeed notice every tire in a parking lot. He admitted to wanting to leave notes on people's cars telling them that they have the wrong tires or that they really need an alignment or to have their tires rotated.

If we immerse ourselves in the words of Scripture, they become a lens through which we can't help but see the world, just as Chet can't help but see cars through the lens of his experience with tires.

When we don't read Scripture, we can feel that God is absent from our lives—we don't hear a voice and we feel alone. But when we read our Bible daily and study it, we begin to hear God speaking to us in everything. There is something powerful about the way God works in us through Scripture reading.

COMMIT TO THE DISCIPLINE

Praying without ceasing is a discipline. Growing in our prayer lives requires a lifelong commitment. Availing ourselves of the precious privilege of gaining wisdom and direction from the Creator of the universe involves the work of establishing a focused and intentional pattern of communication with Him. If we desire to know God's will and feel His presence in the critical moments of our lives, standing at crossroads or enduring dark nights of crisis, then we need to have established a natural and ongoing dialogue.

One of my professors at Talbot School of Theology told a small group of us a story about an evening when God spoke to him while he was in his hot tub. As clear as any voice, he heard God say, "Ask anything for your daughter." He began to cry, and he prayed to God to have his daughter's best friend reach out and connect with her. Their family had relocated for work, and his daughter hadn't heard from her best friend in two years. The very next day his daughter received a call from her.

A noted Christian philosopher once told us a story about how God told him to pull over and pray for his son. At that very moment his son had been in a serious car crash and was fighting for his life.

When we hear stories like that, it's easy to think, *I want that.* But while these stories of unbelievable intimacy with God are exciting, and we want to have that same experience ourselves, what we need to understand is that these moments of urgent clarity are the fruit of a disciplined life of ongoing prayer.

Moments like the ones I just described were exceptions, not the everyday norm; they were the result of an intimacy built up over time. The fruit of prayer is dependent on deep roots, and the more we cultivate and nurture our prayer life, the more we can expect to experience the blessed fruit of clear communication with God.

We must hunger and thirst for such intimacy with God in prayer. We must make it a pattern for our lives. This is why the psalmist could write, "May these words of my mouth and *this meditation of my heart* be pleasing in your sight, LORD, my Rock and my Redeemer" (Psalm 19:14; emphasis added).

It is also why Paul wrote and elaborated to the church in Philippi what sorts of things to think about—"whatever is true, whatever is noble, whatever is right, whatever is pure, whatever is lovely, whatever is admirable."[11]

WHEN WISDOM IS FOLLY

In the paradoxical walk of faith, developing a discipline of close communication with God is critical, and here's why: to the Christian, there are two kinds of wisdom available, and one can look like foolishness from the outside.

Part of God's common grace, available to every human, is the wisdom that comes from reason and experience. As rational beings, we can gather evidence, seek counsel from others, weigh options and likely outcomes, and determine the wisest decision. In this the follower of Christ is on much the same footing as the unbeliever (who is also a rational creature because he is created in God's image). But for those of us who, by entering into the abundant life offered by Christ, have access to communication with our Creator, there may be times when He calls us to something radical and important, something that runs counter to that which normal wisdom would dictate.

When we follow this second form of wisdom, the specific direction from God that only faith can comprehend, our choice may look like folly, as did Abraham's decision to sacrifice his son. At times like that, we must be certain we are hearing God aright; certainty comes from having established the discipline of communicating with Him.

As we run hard after our relationship with God, we are able to grow in wisdom and in our ability to navigate the pitfalls of life. In addition, we are ready and able to hear the occasional call or receive the specific direction that would have us make a radical and disjunctive break from the normal flow of our life, relationships, or conception of our future. As with Abraham, this can only be done in full reliance upon God's trustworthiness and promises of deliverance.

FORWARD IN FAITH OR BACK IN WISDOM

Several years ago I had an adult student at Kilns College who relocated from Idaho to Bend. He and his family moved in the midst of an economic downturn and had left behind a house that continued to sit on the market. As time progressed and they were losing money by paying their mortgage in Idaho and rent in Bend, he began to question whether they should move back to their previous home.

His story is a perfect example of a common scenario in the life of a believer. In the midst of complicated realities, we're left wondering how to analyze our decisions from a biblical standpoint. Generally in these cases, we can either safely move forward in faith or back in wisdom—and we can be obeying God in either option.

Wisdom can mean following natural and spiritual principles that have been proven over time. The reasonableness of some actions or decisions is proven by past experience, one's own and that of others. In other times, when clearly called to do so, we can and should step out in faith, safe with God, by living into the absurdity of trust.

Had God called my friend to Bend? And if so, for what reason? If the Lord had spoken clearly to him on that matter, then it would have been obedient to grab hold of that guidance and step forward in faith. If he hadn't received such specific direction, wisdom and reason might dictate that he consider the complexity of the financial situation, and obedience could mean moving back to the house that hadn't sold.

There is a tension to such discernment and decision making. That which calls us to act rationally can be the voice of God, which we need to obey, or it can be the voice of folly, tempting us to remain safe while ignoring God's trustworthy call to step out in faith. Sometimes when we step out in faith, it flies in the face of wisdom. The art of distinguishing between the two is developed in the steadfast discipline of continuous communication with God.

Be joyful in hope, patient in affliction, faithful in prayer.
—ROMANS 12:12

A WORLD MADE RIGHT

When justice and love are rightly understood, love is not
in conflict with justice but love incorporates justice.[1]
—NICHOLAS WOLTERSTORFF

Shortly after the close of World War II, the newly formed United Nations
convened a group of diverse leaders—headed by Eleanor Roosevelt—and
charged them with a daunting and unprecedented task. They knew from
the outset that they needed to proceed with urgency—the window of
opportunity would be closing fast as the two nations that emerged from the
war as global superpowers would soon be locked into a political, military,
and ideological stalemate that would characterize the second half of the
century. The time was then or never.

The story of the Universal Declaration of Human Rights is a fascinating
one, involving strong personalities with sharp differences of opinion, but
held together by a common goal. In opposing the Axis powers during the
war, the Allies had insisted that massive violations of human dignity—like
those perpetrated by Hitler—be condemned by the larger community of

nations. To give that rhetoric actual force required that the victors create an international bill of rights, a document that would establish standards of human dignity applicable to all people, nations, and governments.

The Declaration was ratified in December 1948 by the UN General Assembly without a single dissenting vote. It has subsequently influenced the concepts found in numerous national constitutions and international treaties. It remains the source document and standard for international humanitarian efforts and organizations to this day. This declaration helped justify the eventual overthrow of apartheid in South Africa and the opposition of the totalitarian regimes of Eastern Europe. It is the foundation for our asylum laws in the United States.

In many respects, however, this effort ran counter to all of previous human history. It had long been the belief and practice that the manner in which a national government treated its own people was its own business, and other nations had no right to interfere. More basically, the unvarying practice throughout the ages was for the powerful to do as they pleased while the weak suffered the consequences. In convening this commission—largely at the insistence of religious and humanitarian groups—and in ratifying this Declaration, the community of nations was both condemning the atrocities that had been witnessed in Europe during Hitler's reign, and giving a voice to the weak and vulnerable for decades into the future in a radically unprecedented way.[2]

We all agree human rights are a good and necessary thing, but what does a story about Eleanor Roosevelt and justice have to do with faith?

THE BIG QUESTION

There is a huge question at the very heart of this conversation about faith and pursuing God. It is the sort of inquiry that must be answered at the onset, or all of our striving is likely to miss the point. It is the big-picture question: *What is God up to?* The answer to this defines and shapes all of our subsequent questions.

What is God's purpose in creation, the incarnation, the Crucifixion, and the resurrection, the calling of disciples, the forming of the church, the giving of the Holy Spirit? What is God's grand scheme, His master plan? What did Jesus mean when He taught His disciples to pray, "Your kingdom come, your will be done, on earth as it is in heaven" (Matthew 6:10)?

Discovering God's will for our own lives can only be grounded in a correct understanding of His will at large. The musician plays best who understands her instrument's role in the entire symphony. The actor carries his part well only to the extent that he understands something of the whole play. Every actor's lines and every instrument's scores are written not for their own sakes but for the contribution they make to the total production.

Yet, perhaps because of the radical individualism of the culture of which we're a part, many Christians seem to miss this truth.

We pray and seek God's will as though He has a specific will for each of us—for each of the seven billion people alive today. I think it's more accurate to understand Him as having *one will* that involves separate roles for each of those seven billion people. Rather than seeing myself as the central figure, I need to learn what the whole puzzle looks like so I can find where my little piece fits.

HARMONIZING RIGHTEOUSNESS

The words *justice* and *righteousness*, although synonyms, have come to mean different things to us in English. *Justice* tends to be applied primarily to matters of criminal justice or legal justice, while righteousness has shifted more and more to mean a form of personal or religious purity.

This means when we come to read these words in our English translations today, we get a different sense than was originally intended by the writers of parts of the Bible or those who translated it into English. In the Greek New Testament, though, there's a single word for both *justice* and *righteousness* (showing the synonymous relationship): δικαιοσύνη.

This word, transliterated *dikaiosune,* was the Greek term for the broadest sense of justice. I possess a tribute coin from the time of Nero that was used to get grain rations in the Roman province around Egypt. It has the word *dikaiosune* on one side and has the goddess Justicia (where we get our Lady Liberty) with scales in one hand and grain in the other hand. In many ways, this is a "social justice" coin from the Roman period around the same time Paul was writing his letter to the Romans.

In numerous passages relevant to the present discussion, because of both the breadth of the original word and how the word *righteousness* has shifted in meaning in modern culture, the use of "righteousness" obscures the impact of what is being written. The classic example comes from Jesus' Sermon on the Mount, specifically, Matthew 5:10: "Blessed are those who are persecuted because of δικαιοσύνη, for theirs is the kingdom of heaven." Most English versions use the word *righteousness* here, but whereas we might be teased for our personal morality, we are not likely to be "persecuted" for it.

Frequently, however, promoting justice and combating injustice exposes one to persecution, since injustice tends to be lucrative for the one perpetrating it. In this passage, as elsewhere, what Jesus had in mind was justice, not morality.

Or what about the beginning of Matthew 6:1–5, where Jesus literally defined the meaning of justice/righteousness in saying, "Be careful not to practice your righteousness in front of others to be seen by them. If you do, you will have no reward from your Father in heaven." Anticipating that His listeners *will* be generous, He continued, "So when you give to the needy, do not announce it with trumpets, as the hypocrites do in the synagogues and on the streets, to be honored by others."

Righteousness here is tied to generosity to the poor. How far is this from the cultural understanding of righteousness as identified with personal purity?

We either have to redefine righteousness to bring it back into alignment with its synonym (*justice*) or we may need to think of translating it as justice.

Imagine how we would understand Jesus' teaching if we read, instead of the translation we're used to, the following: "But seek first his kingdom and his *justice*, and all these things will be given to you as well" (Matthew 6:33). This is of no small importance if we are talking about our biblical understanding of what it means to follow Jesus, be faithful and obedient, and pursue God's will for our lives.

SO WHAT *IS* GOD UP TO?

Understanding God's master plan requires focusing on Jesus and the redemption He came to bring. The Father, Son, and Spirit created a very good universe, and then created a special set of beings with whom to have a special intimacy. Those beings, having free will, chose to write their own score, which had disastrous ramifications for themselves, the rest of the orchestra, and the symphony itself. At a point in space and time, God's Son, Jesus, stepped in to make things right.

We are all familiar with a mission statement. Jesus gave us His mission statement at the public launch of His ministry, in Luke 4, when He applied a famous prophecy from Isaiah to Himself:

> "The Spirit of the Lord is on me,
>   because he has anointed me
>   to proclaim good news to the poor.
> He has sent me to proclaim freedom for the prisoners
>   and recovery of sight for the blind,
> to set the oppressed free,
>   to proclaim the year of the Lord's favor." (vv. 18–19)

Jesus' mission, in His life as well as in His death and resurrection, was to bring about a world made new—a world made *right*—to initiate the process of restoring the whole creation, bringing it back in line with how God intended it to be. And the specific representations of brokenness that Jesus named—as stand-ins for all of the world's brokenness that He came to redress—were the poor, the enslaved, the blind, and the oppressed.

The good news is that God is setting about to make the world right in Christ, and through those who follow Him.

God's plan is that justice would once again prevail on earth, and His will for each of His followers is that they work in concert with Him to that end. That being so, we need to understand justice as central to our walking by faith, as our prayers serve to align our will with God's will for a just world.

Jesus Himself underscored this—and reaffirmed His mission statement—in one of the last recorded speeches before His capture and trial. Here He identified the criterion that He will use at the final judgment to distinguish between those on whom He will bestow His favor and those whom He will reject.

> "Then the King will say to those on his right, 'Come, you who are blessed by my Father; take your inheritance, the kingdom prepared for you since the creation of the world. For I was hungry and you gave me something to eat, I was thirsty and you gave me something to drink, I was a stranger and you invited me in, I needed clothes and you clothed me, I was sick and you looked after me, I was in prison and you came to visit me.'" (Matthew 25:34–36)

The criteria is whether or not we fed and clothed the poor, visited the sick, welcomed the stranger, and visited those in prison. Jesus' criterion is justice.

This is not to say that we gain eternal salvation through what we do. But the clear implication is that those who are themselves made right with God—through Christ's atoning death on the cross—will naturally take up the work Christ came to do, the ministry of reconciliation to which He has called us as His ambassadors.[3]

We don't stray away from good doctrine or truth by focusing on justice and compassion for those in the margins—rather, we find Jesus and truth *in* the margins.

We cannot run after some sort of personal theology that is divorced from a robust and accurate kingdom theology. Yet many of us do. In America, we have come to see peace as a lack of conflict and strife; we define it by reference to what it *excludes* rather than what it *includes*. It is in many ways a negative, rather than a positive, definition. But biblical peace, *shalom*, is a much richer concept. Nicholas Wolterstorff, an eminent Christian philosopher, described it this way:

> I have come to think that ["peace"] is a very poor translation. *Shalom* is flourishing, flourishing in all dimensions of one's existence: in one's relation to God, in one's relation to one's fellow human beings, in one's relation to the natural world, in one's relation to oneself. And over and over when the prophets speak of *shalom*, they make clear that *shalom* requires justice. Human flourishing requires that we treat each other justly.[4]

It is just that sort of justice-laden *shalom* that Jesus came to teach. To follow Him in faith requires our understanding of this, God's master plan.

DEFINING SOCIAL JUSTICE

Let's take a moment to redefine the phrase *social justice*. The most helpful way to think of and define a phrase is to split the words apart. In the case of social justice, it's simply justice with a modifier in front of it. We use modifiers all the time for justice; we speak of *criminal* justice, *international* justice, and *retributive* justice. If we are talking about justice with regard to immigrants, widows and orphans, the poor, or exploited workers—examples of justice *in society*—then "social justice" is an appropriately helpful way to describe it, just as "criminal justice" is descriptive when discussing law and order.

Or look at it this way: truth tells us what *is*; justice tells us *what ought to be*.

Truth and justice are universals. They are hallmark aspects of creation. Accordingly, all the areas of justice—or slices of the justice pie—are necessary because justice itself is necessary.

Justice, therefore, is not just *a* good thing. Rather, justice is a lens by which we look at and evaluate other things. It is a standard God intends to have as a part of His kingdom. Scripture says that justice is the foundation of God's throne (Psalm 89:14) and the scepter by which He rules (Psalm 45:6).

Our understanding of God should compel justice. Conversely, our understanding of justice is one of the ways by which we are meant to understand God more clearly. When we have a greater understanding of God and of justice, we begin to grasp what God is up to in this world.

When a child cares about and participates in something the father does, there is a degree of like-mindedness, understanding, or appreciation that otherwise couldn't be there to the same degree. For example, a son who gets to pack a lunch, grab a fly rod, and go to the river with his dad, who is passionate about fly-fishing, comes to know the heart of his father in a way otherwise not possible. Likewise, when we walk into the world with God, pursuing justice and seeing others and creation through His eyes, we come to know Him better. "For the LORD is a God of justice" (Isaiah 30:18).

Put another way, when we study justice we learn about God. And when we study God we learn about justice. Since justice is rooted in the character of God and flows from the heart of God, they are inseparable.

The question, then, is whether social justice is part of the biblical mandate for justice. In other words, does it fit with what the Bible says about God's justice more broadly?

The answer is a resounding yes.

Social justice has to do with protecting and standing with the vulnerable in society. It is about voluntarily working toward, listening to, empowering, and restoring dignity to every person. Fighting human trafficking, opposing gender violence, caring for AIDS orphans, welcoming the immigrant, and feeding the poor—all these efforts are undergirded by the explicit biblical claim that every person is created in the *image of God*.

Justice is a theological necessity, an ethical imperative, and certainly more than just "another good thing."

For all the tension and debate around the term, what we can't miss is that justice in the social arena—that is, social justice—is part of a biblical justice mandate. We can debate strategies, political platforms, best practices for economics, job creation, and aid programs, but at the end of the day, what is nonnegotiable is God's heart for justice at the center of our cities and as a part of His kingdom. God desires social justice as much as spiritual growth, compassion as much as confession, and sacrificial giving as much as receiving.

JESUS, NOT JUSTICE?

It was after the Friday night of The Justice Conference (2013) in Philadelphia, and a group of about forty nonprofit leaders, pastors, and justice workers were in a hotel suite for an after-party. There was music, deep dialogue, and camaraderie. Then something was said that struck—at least for me—a discordant note.

A young pastor said, "I'm all for justice, but at the end of the day, I want Jesus, not justice."

I'm sure this young pastor had good motives, and that he thought he was being spiritual and getting his priorities straight. Although, like the rest of us, he was working to combat injustice and to follow God's heart for justice, he wanted to make it clear that in the end, he saw justice as a good thing, but not a necessary thing (like Jesus).

In the ensuing conversation, many of the others in the room seemed to agree with him.

Even though I was standing against the wall in the back of the room, my body language must have shown that I was bothered because my friend called out to me and said, "Ken, what do you think?"

I took the next five minutes to correct what I believe is a common category fallacy, and by extension a false dichotomy. The fallacy is pitting two things against each other that are not necessarily opposed. Here is what I told my friends:

In philosophy we make a distinction between *substances* and *properties*. Substances have properties, and properties are possessed by substances.

People are substances, for example, and we have properties too: I have the property of being five foot ten, being a husband and a father, being the son of John and Bonnie Wytsma, being intuitive in personality type, and being American in nationality.

Some properties are essential to what makes up the substance or person, and others are less important. As horrific as it would be, if I lost my right leg in a car crash, I'd still be Ken Wytsma. If, on the other hand, you tried to remove from me that I am a father or the son of John and Bonnie—you would no longer be talking about Ken Wytsma. These are essential and defining characteristics of me.

We are told in 1 John 4:8, "Anyone who does not love does not know God, because God is love" (ESV). Love—a property—is so closely associated with God—a substance[5]—that the substance cannot be known apart from entering into possession of the property love.

It is the same with Jesus and justice. Jesus is a substance, whereas justice is a property. And this particular property, justice, is an essential attribute of Jesus, so closely identified with Him as to make it incoherent to think of Him as separate from this property.

Remember, Jesus' mission statement was all about justice, and social justice in particular. The psalmist wrote, "The LORD is known by his . . . justice" (Psalm 9:16). In Isaiah 59:14–20, Jesus (the Messiah/Redeemer) is identified as God's own right arm of justice.

Justice was Jesus' mission, what He did in healing people and advocating for the poor, and the mandate He left His followers—that we should do likewise, and love one another. In fact, justice and Jesus are so closely linked that whatever we do for the poor, vulnerable, or oppressed is as if we are doing it literally *to* Him and *for* Him.

Justice is an essential attribute of Jesus that affects everything—our ethics, our relationships, and our ability to attain intimacy with Him. Put another way, there has never been a time in history where Jesus was present and justice was not. There never will be a time—in the future of the world or in your own life—where God's Holy Spirit is at work while justice is absent. You can't have "Jesus, not justice." They are inseparable. Pitting the two against each other is a category fallacy (these two things being comple-mentary) and a false dichotomy. They are not simply words on cardboard squares: one with the letters J-E-S-U-S and the other with J-U-S-T-I-C-E, that we choose between. This isn't a question of grammatical priority or which vocabulary word is most important. Forcing a choice between the two is unnecessary and oversimplifies the dynamic nature of Jesus—not as a word, but as a person.

Where Jesus is, justice is present. Justice is at the heart of who He is. Justice is a priority because Jesus came to bring about a world made right.

I'm not sure if everyone in the room that night in Philadelphia caught the argument, but it is one I believe is important if we are to correct false perceptions about justice and its relation to our calling and God's will for our lives.

JUSTICE AS A BAD LIFE STRATEGY

There's some bad news involved in discovering what God is up to. Engaging in justice—and especially, seeking to redress injustice—is not the shortest route to fulfilling the American Dream.

In material terms, in terms of personal comfort and ease, living justly is likely to be counterproductive. At least in a human economy, generosity does not pad one's own bank account. Stopping to help someone else takes time away from one's own pursuit of leisure, or pleasure, or financial gain.

As just one example, consider the issue of immigration and immigra-tion reform. In the United States, and even in the church in America, there has been persistent opposition to any legal reforms that would facilitate the process by which currently undocumented immigrants could attain citizenship or legal status. This is despite the fact that nearly all of us are the descendants of immigrants and that throughout Scripture God explic-itly demonstrates that immigrants have a special place in His heart and economy.[6]

The arguments generally given against such reforms all revolve around the question, "How will this affect me or my bottom line?" and the conclusion that they (immigrants) will somehow inconvenience me.

It's true; doing the just thing can often be inconvenient. This is likely why God in Scripture repeatedly commands His people to care for the immigrant, because He knows that the possibility of inconvenience will otherwise cause people to abdicate their responsibility to the strangers among them. Inconvenience is no justification at all for not acting justly.

But more than convenience, comfort and personal security often may be at stake. In fact, combating injustice can be very risky business, dangerous to one's health and life. Centuries before Christ, Plato wrote (in book 2 of *Republic*) that "the truly just person will be crucified." Gaining equal rights for black Americans cost Martin Luther King Jr. and many others their lives. Nelson Mandela's battle to abolish apartheid meant twenty-seven years in prison.

All over the world today, those engaged in heeding Christ's call to be His hands and feet to "the least of these"[7] are fully cognizant that this entails risks both known and unforeseen.

WHEN DREAMS GET IN THE WAY

As a leader, I am often inundated by Christian leadership books and essays on goal setting and life planning (having a bucket list of what I hope to do before I die).

Bucket lists can be idolatrous, however—things that can end up driving us instead of God's direction for us. Idols are incredibly dangerous because they reshape the entirety of lives.

I have a friend, Keith, who followed God into some of the poorest places in the world by putting on hold education, business ventures, and even involvement with the US rugby team. But what if he had been guided by the thought, *I want to see Rome, climb the Himalayas, drive a motorcycle down Route 66, and retire to a lake home in Wyoming before I die*? Would he have ended up running a relief and development organization years later, helping millions of people in poverty? Would he have an adopted daughter whom God brought into the life of his family while ministering overseas?

Sometimes dreams or overly defined life goals can get in the way of God's plans. Certainly, God can use goals, and often does, but we always have to hold them in loose hands, recognizing that God could want us to head a different direction, or stop short of reaching a goal, or do something that would make all of our dreams and goals unattainable because of how God chooses to use us.

This brings us right back to the issue of walking in faith and surfaces another paradox.

THE JUST SHALL LIVE BY FAITH

A common theme in the Old and New Testaments is that "the just shall live by faith."[8] Why is it that the just person must live by faith?

It is simply this: if we are not looking out for ourselves, then we have to trust that God is looking out for us. If—in following Christ's call on us to give our lives away on behalf of the voiceless oppressed—we have to put ourselves in places and situations over which we have little or no control, then we have to lean into God's sovereignty. If God's direction takes us through unhealthy or dangerous paths, we can only move forward in full reliance upon Him.

It is a paradox—albeit one clearly stated by Jesus Himself and later by His disciple John and His apostle Paul[9]—that the person who wants to find true life must first be willing to lay it down, to die to self. But the blessing in the paradox is this: as we give over control to God, He *will* look after us.

"The just will live by faith" simply states the obvious: that if I live outside of myself, if I live to give and serve, if I think of others as being as important as myself, if I live for justice—what ought to be—I have to trust that somehow I am going to be taken care of. I have to believe that it truly is better to give than receive, and that God really does watch over and sustain the just.

This is not to say that God's will for our individual lives is of supreme importance, much less that obedience to His call will mean that He preserves us from sickness, suffering, or even death. But we can be assured that only as we take our rightful place in His master plan can we find the path to all the blessing He has in store for us.

Eleanor Roosevelt, who spent her later years immersed in the creation of a document that furthered the cause of justice all over the world, prayed the following prayer every night:

> Our Father, who has set a restlessness in our hearts and made us all seekers after that which we can never fully find, forbid us to be satisfied with what we make of life. Draw us from base content and set our eyes on far-off goals. Keep us at tasks too hard for us that we may be driven to Thee for strength. Deliver us from fretfulness and self-pitying: make us sure of the good we cannot see and of the hidden good in the world. Open our eyes to simple beauty all around us and our hearts to the loveliness men hide from us because we do not try to understand them. Save us from ourselves and show us a vision of a world made new.[10]

Jesus is out to set our world right. Because our world is not right, we are faced with the tension of the way things are (truth) and the way they ought to be (justice). In Christian discipleship, therefore, joining Jesus' justice project means stepping out in faith and relishing the paradox—finding our lives as we're giving them away.

For the Lord loves the just and will not forsake his faithful ones.
—Psalm 37:28

VIRTUE, THE GREEKS, AND THE MEANING OF HAPPINESS

All that we call human history   money, poverty, ambition,
war, prostitution, classes, empires, slavery—[is] the
long terrible story of man trying to find something
other than God which will make him happy.[1]
—C. S. Lewis

We Americans identify happiness with feelings, the sort of emotion we find in a bag of popcorn and a DVD with a happy ending.

I can still remember the exact moment when I came to think that the things I most wanted in life were pleasure and happiness. It was early in high school, and I was watching the movie *Dead Poets Society* with some friends. The theme of the movie was contained in the phrase *Carpe diem* and in Henry David Thoreau's explanation of why he went out to Walden Pond—to "suck out all the marrow of life."[2] The idea of seizing the day and getting the most out of life resonated deep within me and became my unofficial creed. Much of my generation likely shared this motivating belief.

What resulted from this approach, however, was not happiness. As a life strategy, the pursuit of *pleasure* (in Greek, *hedone*) has so regularly been tried and found to fail, that philosophers have a name for this phenomenon—the *hedonistic paradox*. The hedonistic paradox is that when you pursue pleasure for its own sake, you tend not to find it.

As a new believer, I sat down to write out the meaning of life. I only made it two pages. I realized that there was so little I understood on the subject, which gave me a hunger to go deeper on the big questions surrounding purpose, the meaning of life, and happiness. I began taking philosophy classes and set a course for graduate school.

In the spring before beginning graduate studies, while I was still trying to decide where to attend, I visited Biola University in Southern California. The admissions counselor set up a meeting for me with J. P. Moreland. I still remember that meeting as if it were yesterday. It was a thirty-minute slot over his lunch break, and we met in his small, windowless office. His desk was full of books and writing projects in process, and the shelves lining every wall were crowded with books two deep. Dr. Moreland was warm and friendly, and he seemed genuinely glad to meet me, but I could tell he was busy and thinking I was just one more student coming through the college. When I brought up the subject of happiness, however, his eyes lit up. He took his feet off his desk, leaned forward in his chair (yogurt in hand), and began to talk wildly about the true nature and meaning of happiness, its classical roots, and the tragedy of losing this understanding in modern Christian thought.

It was at that moment that I decided to attend Talbot School of Theology, a graduate school at Biola University, and to pursue a master's degree in philosophy and Christian thought.

Eventually, I came to realize that the hedonistic myth involved a misaligned focus. It's not that happiness *per se* is wrong, but that we tend to misunderstand the true source of happiness. God designed us in such a way that our happiness and fulfillment are to be identified with righteous movement. Our pursuit of God and our pursuit of true happiness, rightly understood, *are one and the same.*

RECLAIMING HAPPINESS

While at Talbot, I read *Confessions* by Augustine. I found his writing more relevant than anything I'd ever read, and one sentence in particular was a wake-up call: "For you have made us for yourself, and our heart is restless till it finds its rest in you."[3] Instead of running from God to attain happiness, happiness is found in running toward God.

Happiness, instead of being a selfish pursuit, as many Christians unknowingly feel, is a godly pursuit.

But we have diluted the true meaning of happiness. These days, happiness often means a license to pursue *self*-gratification. It wasn't always defined this way, however. Aristotle defined happiness as the chief end of humans and saw it extending throughout one's life. As he wrote, "Moreover it must be in a complete life. For one swallow does not make a spring, nor does one day; nor, similarly, does one day or a short time make us blessed and happy."[4]

His view of happiness included character development and the attainment of all other virtues. Achieving happiness meant fulfilling one's potential in a holistic, ethical way.

For Aristotle and many of the ancients, happiness was a state of being; they used the word much as we use the word *joy.* Aristotle's unabashed use of happiness as a driving force for doing good and being ethical was picked up by many Christian scholars at least through the Enlightenment. Augustine, Thomas Aquinas, and later Blaise Pascal all saw happiness, rightly defined, as one of the ends of human life; they saw no tension between happiness and living for God.

When Thomas Jefferson penned the phrase "the pursuit of happiness" in the Declaration of Independence, he, too, had in mind the classical sense of the word *happiness.* Drawing from the traditions of ancient Greek philosophers (and modifying a statement by John Locke[5]), Jefferson saw true *happiness*—the full development of human potential—as a human right and goal alongside *life* and *liberty*.

It wasn't until recently that the word *happiness* has been watered down to simply mean *pleasure* without regard to ethics or virtue. But this watering down explains why present-day Christians unknowingly have a hard time considering the word *happiness* in a positive light, and an even harder time thinking of it as something connected to faith, righteousness, justice, and obedience.

COMPLETE JOY

Why is it we often feel our selfish desires are in conflict with our holy desires? We see in Scripture that God's design for the unity of our desires is found in pursuing right relationship with Him and others. Dissolving that unity, or separating our desires from our actions, results in an anemic faith and tempers the passion that is properly appointed for obedience.

There are two ways we can seek happiness. We can seek it for ourselves at the expense of others, or we can seek it on behalf of others. The second is the kingdom happiness Jesus calls "complete" joy that lacks nothing, the kind that produces right actions and genuine love.

Jesus said, "As the Father has loved me, so have I loved you. Now remain in my love. If you obey my commands, you will remain in my love, just as I have obeyed my Father's commands and remain in his love. I have told you this *so that my joy may be in you and that your joy may be complete*" (John 15:9–11; emphasis added).

The reality is that our happiness, God's glory, and loving our neighbors are all bound together. Understanding this, we can pursue an obedient faith in a holistic way, expecting to experience new heights in both our relationship with God and our own flourishing and satisfaction. Without this understanding, we've missed something important in our faith—in our pursuit of justice, godliness, and joy.

It's counterintuitive.

As the last chapter tried to show, living for God includes living for justice. Here, the argument is that living for God and for justice (our sacrifice for others) is somehow tied up with our own happiness. Or, as Jesus put the paradox, it truly is better to give than to receive.

As we give our lives away, we receive life back. Happiness is a reward for living justly.

Jesus gave us a further picture of godly happiness in His Sermon on the Mount in what we call the Beatitudes (Matthew 5:1–12). The word *Beatitudes* is taken from the Latin word *beati*—meaning "power," "blessed," or "happy." And *beati* is a translation of the Greek word *makarios* that was in the original version of Matthew, a word that also meant "happy," "blessed," or even "to be envied." Jesus' words indicate that while those who are meek, merciful, peacemakers, and persecuted may not have pleasure in the moment, they are the ones who will find true happiness and blessing from God the Father.

We need to recover the full, classical sense of the word *happiness*, because happiness is a vital part of the conversation about faith. Though there is a corrupted happiness that hampers active faith, there is also a happiness that spurs us onward, a happiness that brings community together and helps establish an intimate relationship with God. Happiness is the current that helps carry us along, and happiness, as strange as it may seem, provides a natural and godly motivation for doing good.

ENTITLEMENT

One thing that gets in the way of our pursuit of God and godly happiness is a feeling of entitlement, an idea that we have more rights than we actually do.

Every person has a variety of rights—rights endowed by God, rights conferred through citizenship, rights to be respected according to the status and place one has earned, rights within families, and so forth. The sum total of these rights constitutes a line to which we are entitled.

But we go beyond this line; we feel we have rights to a new car, more money, new clothes, getting our own way, a bigger house, have God appease our strongest felt needs, vent our frustrations without maturity, or act on our impulses childishly. These are not things to which we are actually entitled, but to which we often *feel* strongly entitled.

The inflation or gap between real and perceived entitlement can largely be attributed to lack of maturity or being "spoiled." It may be the way we were raised or just the prevailing American consumer culture, but we tend to believe we deserve more than we actually do.

This gap, however it occurs in individual persons, tends to eat away at cheerfulness and gratitude, often while nurturing a *victim complex* or feelings that life is not fair in that it has not provided one with all he or she deserves.

THE HUNTINGTON LIBRARY

One of the dominant illustrations of entitlement and contentment in my life occurred when I was walking around the Huntington Library in Pasadena, California. The Huntington Library is the estate of the late Henry E. Huntington, a railroad tycoon in early California history whose name is also given to Huntington Beach. His estate was turned into a collection of museums, libraries, and gardens. It's one of my favorite places in Los Angeles—the botanical gardens create an oasis spanning 120 acres within the urban landscape of L.A.

The gardens reflect those of different places around the world: there are the Japanese Garden, the Palm Garden, and the Desert Garden, to name a few. By the teahouse and Rose Garden, where the rosebushes include every variety, there is a covered walkway with ivy running through the latticework. There's something about light streaming through the covered walkway, the sense of age and peace that comes from the vines growing in and around the lattice, that speaks my language and is beautiful to me.

On a gorgeous day, one of my first times to the library, I remember walking through the archway and thinking, *If only I could own this. If only this place could be mine. If only I could come stroll here in the evenings and be able to enjoy this all to myself. If only I wasn't a visitor here, but could fold this into the things that belong to me. Then I could really enjoy this.*

It was a bit of a scary thought to realize what was going on in my mind, to recognize that the need to possess was somehow standing in the way of my enjoyment.

THE SECRET OF CONTENTMENT

Feelings of entitlement can be overcome by pursuing godly contentment and living lives in submission to the One who created us. Contentment does not result from accumulating more and more stuff, or from reaching the upper line of a *perceived* entitlement. It also does not come from having the bare minimum of the lower line of *actual* entitlement. Rather, true joy and contentment come through spiritual strength and encouragement that transcend our lot in life, the sum total of our possessions, and whether or not we are receiving all we think we deserve.

Paul talked about learning the secret of being content whether he had plenty or nothing at all in the fourth chapter of the letter to the Philippians. He attributed the source of contentment to Christ by saying, "I can do all this through him who gives me strength" (v. 13).

It has been a consistent recognition by Christians throughout church history that we were created for relationship with God, and that only in that relationship do we find contentment. Thomas Aquinas wrote, "God alone constitutes [our] happiness."[6] C. S. Lewis has Aslan reassure Caspian, in his work *Prince Caspian,* with the words, "You come of the Lord Adam and the Lady Eve. And that is both honor enough to erect the head of the poorest beggar, and shame enough to bow the shoulders of the greatest emperor on earth. Be content."[7]

I think contemporary pastor and theologian John Piper summarized the idea of finding our happiness in God best: "God is most pleased with us when we are most satisfied in Him."[8]

That is why when it comes to true happiness, prayer is more fruitful than striving, solitude more beneficial than competition, and trusting more reliable than claiming entitlements.

Where I worked at a manufacturing plant in South Carolina, there was a framed plaque on the wall with a quote from Pastor Chuck Swindoll. This short piece, entitled "Attitude," sums up the idea of a contented spirit as well as anything I've ever seen. I have shared it multiple times with my church and have also begun teaching it to my daughters.

> The longer I live, the more I realize the impact of attitude on life. Attitude, to me, is more important than facts. It is more important than the past, than education, than money, than circumstances, than failures, than successes, than what other people think, say or do. It is more important than appearance, giftedness or skill. It will make or break a company . . . a church . . . a home. The remarkable thing is we have a choice every day regarding the attitude we embrace for that day. We cannot change our past . . . we cannot change the fact that people will act in a certain way. We cannot change the inevitable. The only thing we can do is play the one string we have, and that is our attitude . . . I am convinced that life is 10% what happens to me and 90% how I react to it. And so it is with you . . . we are in charge of our attitudes.

Contentment does not depend on having; it depends on our heart's wanting the right things. As C. S. Lewis put it, "our best havings are wantings."[9] I would rather be able to appreciate things I cannot have than to have things I am not able to appreciate.

Of course, one of the greatest enemies of contentment is envy. My best suggestion for combating envy is this: when tempted to compare yourself with those who have more, give yourself instead to those who have less.

LIVING IN THE TENSION

There is a tension to spiritual happiness. It is the paradox that while our felt needs and fears are closely tied to circumstances, happiness is somehow meant to transcend those needs, fears, and circumstances. But in the midst of bad circumstances, *how do you consider your trials pure joy?*

As with Peter walking on water, it's really hard to keep our eyes on the source that sustains our faith, and it's easy to focus instead on the many challenges or obstacles to walking in trust. Biblical happiness can ground itself in faith; it can exist alongside a bad day or a bad week, or even in the face of bad news. A basic difference between biblical happiness and pleasure is this: the existence of pleasure depends upon your immediate circumstances and emotional state, whereas biblical happiness and contentment can exist even when your present circumstances are difficult or challenging and your natural emotional state tenuous and volatile.

Life is messy. God is mysterious. And the successful quest for happiness will be a spiritual one. Happiness and the good life are for the Christian the same end as for the various schools of ancient philosophy. For the Christian, however, they are to be found in the virtues of a relationship with God.

Several hundred years ago, Pascal wrote of man's inescapable need for God. Connecting our happiness with dependence upon God, he wrote,

> There was once in man a true happiness, of which all that now remains is the empty print and trace. This he tries in vain to fill with everything around him, seeking in things that are not there the help he cannot find in those that are, though none can help, since this infinite abyss can be filled only with an infinite and immutable object; in other words by God himself.[10]

This biblical understanding of happiness can seem like a mere platitude or abstract concept, but it ought to be the goal of every disciple of Christ to experience it as a fundamental reality of the walk of faith. What is more, when we learn to orient our desires away from circumstances and material things and toward relationship with God, we discover that true happiness far surpasses the sort of happiness for which we used to long. C. S. Lewis said:

> If we consider the unblushing promises of reward and the staggering nature of the rewards promised in the Gospels, it would seem that our

Lord finds our desire not too strong, but too weak. We are half-hearted creatures, fooling about with drink and sex and ambition when infinite joy is offered us, we are like ignorant children who want to continue making mud pies because we cannot imagine what is meant by the offer of a vacation at the sea. We are far too easily pleased.[11]

"I have come that they may have life, and have it to the full."
—John 10:10

7

DOUBT

Doubt is a pain too lonely to know that faith is his twin brother.[1]
—KHALIL GIBRAN

I once taught a class called the History and Philosophy of Atheism, which I could easily have called the History of Doubt. Atheism is essentially the story of what we don't know about God or what we're unsure about.

There are two types of doubt in our culture: honest doubt and stupid doubt. Stupid doubt is trendy, stylish doubt. It's the kind of doubt that is more about feeling smart, feeling powerful, or giving yourself license to do what you want.

In Western culture, it's trendy to doubt and be skeptical. In fact, people who claim certainty or truth are viewed as extremists. Dallas Willard said it this way: "For centuries now our culture has cultivated the idea that the *skeptical* person is always smarter than one who believes. You can be almost as stupid as a cabbage, as long as you doubt."[2]

Stupid doubt is the kind of doubt celebrities like to flaunt on late-night talk shows. It's the same kind a friend of mine has when she chuckles at any mention of spiritual things. It's the doubt that uses the actions of violent extremists and political powers as evidence against the validity of ancient texts and religions. It's the kind that manifests in stupid questions like "If God is all-powerful, could He create a rock so heavy He couldn't move it?" It's the doubt that thrives on social media.

But honest doubt is different. Honest doubt is true, authentic uncertainty about what you believe or what you want to believe.

For example, Elie Wiesel is a holocaust survivor, Nobel Peace Prize winner, and author who was instrumental in the creation of the National Holocaust Museum in Washington, DC. He penned *The Trial of God* and many others, which are full of honest doubt—the kind of doubt many holocaust survivors faced and continue to face. Doubt experienced when God seems distant—or worse, nonexistent.

Far from being proud of our honest doubts, we're often a little embarrassed by them. They eat away at our confidence in things about which we long for certainty.

We begin to have honest doubts when we:

- encounter the complexity of the universe
- confront evil in the world
- discover evil in ourselves
- feel lost or broken
- can't find God
- are overcome by guilt

IN DESPAIR

When it comes to Christianity, we tend to struggle with doubt in two different ways. I see it as two slopes on either side of a tall peak. The peak is our experience of God, where we find certainty of both His presence and love.

However, leading up to the peak there is a slope of skepticism or intellectual doubt known by some of us when we first wrestle with the idea that God exists. For someone who was raised in a loving Christian home, this slope might be less steep or nonexistent. For someone who was raised in an atheistic home, has long lived in an atheistic environment, or has grown up in a difficult or abusive Christian home, this peak can be *very* steep.

The other kind of doubt is the descending slope. It tends to sneak up on us and surprise us. After we've had an experience of God and felt a degree of certainty that He is real and loves us, something or someone happens to us, and our certainty begins to erode away. We wake up one morning, and there is doubt.

Doubt on the descending slope tends to come from three places: injustice, pain, and distance.

WHERE IS GOD? THE WORLD IS DYING!

One of the loudest—and most emotionally compelling—claims against Christianity is this: How can a loving and powerful God allow so much hatred, evil, and suffering to go on in the world? Why do good things happen to bad people and bad things happen to good people? Why do oppressors prosper and victims suffer?

This complaint is nothing new. The ancient Greek philosopher Epicurus taught that we should only believe things we can directly experience or measure, and that morality should be as simple as maximizing pleasure and minimizing pain for oneself and others.[3] He summed up the claim against God's justice thousands of years ago: "Is God willing to prevent evil, but not able? Then he is not omnipotent. Is he able, but not willing? Then he is malevolent. Is he both able and willing? Then whence cometh evil? Is he neither able nor willing? Then why call him God?"[4]

These are powerful questions.

If you go to the Bible to find answers to those questions, you may walk away disappointed. What you will find is a whole lot of other people asking the same questions. For example, look at Jeremiah 12:1:

> You are always righteous, LORD,
>   when I bring a case before you.
> Yet I would speak with you about your justice:
>   Why does the way of the wicked prosper?
>   Why do all the faithless live at ease?

And Psalm 73 from Asaph:

> For I was envious of the arrogant
> As I saw the prosperity of the wicked.
> For there are no pains in their death,
> And their body is fat.
> They are not in trouble as other men,
> Nor are they plagued like mankind. . . .
> They mock and wickedly speak of oppression . . .
>
> Surely in vain I have kept my heart pure
> And washed my hands in innocence;
> For I have been stricken all day long
> And chastened every morning. (vv. 3–5, 8, 13–14 NASB)

Jesus even leaned into this idea in Matthew 5:45: "For he makes his sun rise on the evil and on the good, and sends rain on the just and on the unjust" (ESV).

The unfairness and injustice in the world create tension for us. We begin to demand that God defend Himself. This has been such a problem throughout history that there's actually a philosophical term for an argument reconciling the existence of God with the existence of evil: it is called a *theodicy*. The word *theodicy* is a combination of the Greek words for *God* and *justice* and literally means "a justification of God."

WHERE IS GOD WHEN I'M HURTING?

Objective evil is only the tip of the iceberg. The stakes become much higher when we personally experience injustice, unfairness, or suffering.

Job is always the classic biblical picture of suffering, and the Psalms are full of laments and cries from God's people who feel alone and separated from God. But what about the nation of Israel in Egypt? We have all probably heard the story in Exodus of the children of Israel and how they cried out in their slavery: "During those many days the king of Egypt died, and the people of Israel groaned because of their slavery and cried out for help" (Exodus 2:23 ESV).

When we hear that verse, we know how the story ends. We know that God is about to deliver them through Moses. But listen to the prophecy God told Abraham many years before: "Know for certain that your offspring will be sojourners in a land that is not theirs and will be servants there, and they will be afflicted for *four hundred years*" (Genesis 15:13 ESV; emphasis added).

When we read the Exodus story, we imagine a group of people crying out in their suffering and then being delivered. Deliverance was the answer to their fear, suffering, and doubt. But what about all the generations that came before who were born into slavery and died in slavery? What was the answer to their pain? Did God not hear their cries?

Look at the opening of Malachi: "'I have loved you,' says the Lord. 'But you ask, "How have you loved us?"'" (1:2).

Isn't that how suffering feels? We want to say, "You claim to love me, God, but where's the love?"

Pain can make pessimists out of us. It clouds our ability to see goodness anywhere, especially the goodness of God. The more suffering we experience, the farther we feel from God. As we feel farther and farther from Him, we lose hope and begin to doubt.

WHERE IS GOD?

At the core, we are worried that God is not really there, or that He does not really like us or care about us. But when we look at the Psalms, we discover that the hiddenness of God is not a new problem.

> O God, you are my God; earnestly I seek you;
>> my soul thirsts for you;
>> my flesh faints for you,
>> as in a dry and weary land where there is no water. (Psalm 63:1 ESV)

> Save me, O God!
>> For the waters have come up to my neck.
>> I sink in deep mire
>> where there is no foothold;
>> I have come into deep waters,
>> and the flood sweeps over me.
>> I am weary with crying out;
>> my throat is parched. My eyes grow dim
>> with waiting for my God. (Psalm 69:1–3 ESV)

Psalm 88 is one of the most visceral, plainspoken passages in the Old Testament:

> O LORD, God of my salvation;
>> I cry out day and night before you.
>> Let my prayer come before you;
>> incline your ear to my cry!

For my soul is full of troubles,
and my life draws near to Sheol.
I am counted among those who go down to the pit;
I am a man who has no strength,
like one set loose among the dead,
like the slain that lie in the grave,
like those whom you remember no more,
for they are cut off from your hand. . . .
Do you work wonders for the dead?
Do the departed rise up to praise you? . . .
Are your wonders known in the darkness,
or your righteousness in the land of forgetfulness?
But I, O Lord, cry to you;
in the morning my prayer comes before you.
O Lord, why do you cast my soul away?
Why do you hide your face from me? . . .
You have caused my beloved and my friend to shun me;
my companions have become darkness. (vv. 1–5, 10, 12–14, 18
esv)

We live in a broken world where suffering is a guarantee. We can be rent by life, stress, tragedy, sin, a persuasive argument against our beliefs, or even something disturbing we read in the Bible. We all experience moments, even seasons of doubt.

I was once in a long, serious meeting with a group of pastors, and during a break, this question came up: "What are you afraid of?" A fairly well-known pastor, to whom all the other pastors in the group looked up, said, honestly: "I hope it's all true. I hope I don't find out someday that this was all a fairy tale or some elaborate hoax." Everybody was shocked. Pastors are not supposed to doubt that God exists or that Christianity is true. I couldn't get his answer out of my mind for days. That confession of doubt is one of the most authentic things I have ever heard a pastor say.

That pastor echoes the aching of the Psalms, and both attest to this: the hiddenness of God is only an argument against Him if we do not expect God to be hidden. But all throughout Scripture, God is spoken of as a hide-and-seek God, meaning that often God is hidden, yet we are supposed to continually seek after Him. It is comforting to know that in Scripture and all throughout church history, godly men and women have struggled to sense the presence of God or to understand why He would allow certain things to occur in our lives.

If doubt is an unavoidable part of the human condition, we are going to have to learn how to navigate through it if we want to live a life of faith.

ANSWERS WON'T HELP

Doubt creates a desperation for answers. We really convince ourselves that answers are our way out of doubt. If I could just understand

- the violence in the Old Testament . . .
- the doctrine of the Trinity . . .
- how salvation works . . .
- the way science and the Bible fit together . . .
- why Christians have done such horrible things in the past . . .
- why this is happening to me . . .
- why I lost my job . . .
- why my son is dying . . .

But even if God gave us a perfect, logical answer, would it take away the emotional experience? Would it really change the way we feel and answer our doubts as perfectly as we want?

When I was a college pastor, I used to put on an event called the Skeptics Ball, which eventually grew into the website AskQuestions.tv. It was an evening get-together opened up for any questions. Any topic. Any question. The goal was to make space for people to raise their doubts and critiques of Christianity or the Bible and get an answer or, at the least, honest dialogue.

One night in particular sticks in my memory. On the second floor of a brick church that had been baking in the July sun all day, forty or fifty people were crammed into a tiny room with a low ceiling. I couldn't tell whether the hot breeze coming through the open windows was making it better or worse.

I had been answering questions for an hour, and I was melting in the heat and drained from the mental exertion of the evening. There was a small stack of anonymous, handwritten questions next to me, and when I picked one up, my heart sank. The question was: "Why would God allow rape?" It is a pretty gnarly question on its own, but I knew who had asked it. A teenage girl in the church had been raped only weeks before . . . and her parents were sitting in the back row. What was I supposed to say?

The objective answer to suffering is stark and unfeeling: "The world is broken; you are not the first, you are not the only, and you won't be the last to suffer. But God is good." While I honestly believe that is true, it is not going to make anyone feel better or change that person's experience. And it is not really the point, is it?

There is a better answer: the subjective answer. The answer that dignifies the suffering person. The answer that empathizes in an effort to understand and share in the suffering.

The subjective answer changes everything: "You are not alone; you are not forgotten; you are loved. By God, by me, by your church community. And we are hurting alongside you." It recognizes that no cute phrase, Bible verse, song, book, tract, or sermon will change what someone is going through or reverse his or her experience. It takes responsibility for the suffering of the person, caring for and bearing the pain alongside that individual.

It was in that moment, as I stood, a bit panicked, with my pulse pounding in my forehead, wondering whether it was better to make eye contact or to avoid it, that I realized: there was no cold, hard, factual answer to relieve that family's suffering. But the girl's family was not in need of an explanation for what happened to them. They had experienced evil and were in need of love. Love from God, their family, their friends, and their church community. A logical answer about the goodness of God or the problem of evil could not change the girl's experience . . . but love could.

In the midst of suffering, answers don't change the experience: love changes the experience.

THE HOUSE OF CARDS

I have always found this interesting: one of the critiques atheists level at Christians is that religion is a crutch, a placebo to make us feel better about the difficulty of life. The odd thing is that in my experience suffering and evil often cause Christians their greatest degree of doubt.

Our certainty will often come crashing down around our ears when we are under stress or hurting—no matter what we believe. Truth remains the same, whether it feels true or not. Anybody can be hammered by doubt. To think we'll never doubt is naive. Everyone has a breaking point.

I was talking once to a friend when I pictured two soldiers side by side in a foxhole in World War II. Bullets zipping overhead, bombs exploding all around them, and they are the only two men in their company left alive.

One of the soldiers was born and raised a Christian, the other a dyed-in-the-wool atheist. I could easily see the atheist praying a desperate prayer to God, just in case He was there. I could also see the Christian suddenly overcome by doubt about the existence of heaven and life after death.

One of C. S. Lewis's most famous books is *The Problem of Pain*, a philosophical book that defends God and attempts to explain suffering. Lewis wrote it in his forties, and it displays a powerful intellectual grasp of the reality and nature of suffering. But it wasn't the only book he would write on the subject of pain.

He waited nearly his entire life to meet his wife—they were married the year he turned fifty-nine. But she died three short years later. He had all the answers to why people die and why bad things happen, but that didn't prepare him for the experience of losing his best friend and spouse.

The unfairness and injustice of so quickly losing the woman he had waited sixty years to meet nearly broke Lewis. He poured out his grief and doubt in a journal that was published after his death as *A Grief Observed*.

Read what he had to say about his faith:

> God has not been trying an experiment on my faith or love in order to find out their quality. He knew it already. It was I who didn't. In this trial He makes us occupy the dock, the witness box, and the bench all at once. He always knew that my temple was a house of cards. His only way of making me realize the fact was to knock it down.[5]

It's almost as though a different Lewis wrote that paragraph. The younger Lewis wrote about pain objectively—the elder Lewis wrestled with it experientially. I had a professor once say, "Wounds are deeper than our convictions." Lewis didn't live the rest of his life in a state of doubt, but for me his "house of cards" has always illustrated that even the person with the most intellectual faith can be laid low by their emotions and personal experience.

In 2007, a collection of Mother Teresa's private letters was published, called *Mother Teresa: Come Be My Light*.[6] The letters, which were never intended to be read by the public, reveal that she occasionally experienced deep personal torment and periods of intense doubt. This revelation, the personal doubts and fears of someone many consider a saint, surprised many. To me, it only showed her humanity and the fact that we all—even the saints—share struggle and doubt in common.

Christianity is not a crutch. Real Christians living by faith, looking for more than a security blanket or a genie in a bottle, demand more than a spiritual crutch to make them feel good about ultimate reality. Christians actually require a level of personal engagement and love from God far beyond the intellectual proposition that He exists and loves them. Maybe that's why Jude said, "Be merciful to those who doubt" (v. 22).

FAITH IS THE ANSWER

Faith isn't destroyed or diminished by doubt. The opposite is true: faith is the *answer* to doubt.

When you are in the desert and are dying of thirst, collapsing in the sand won't take you to water. When you are drowning in the ocean, becoming motionless won't save your life. Why when we are doubting do we often believe that bringing our Christian walk to a halt will provide us with answers? We get hung up by our doubt, refusing to move forward until we have answers.

Sometimes we inadvertently or even deliberately hit the brakes to create distance between us and God. That's why turning to sin in the midst of doubt is such a bad idea. The progression often goes like this: we get hurt and say something like, "I am really struggling with my faith. I need a break from church for a while." Usually that also means a break from prayer, a break from the Bible, and a general break from our Christian community and even our moral code.

But if we were to be honest and say what's really going on, it might sound more like, "I'm not sure God exists or loves me. So I'm going to isolate myself from Him, His Word, and all the people I know who believe in Him. Instead, I'll turn to the things I know will give me satisfaction and pleasure until I feel happy enough to believe in God again."

How can we expect to find God by deliberately pushing Him away? We all understand that cheating on your spouse isn't going to solve marital problems. It may bring satisfaction for a while, but it certainly won't fix any problems. Instead, it will most likely be catalytic in the ultimate destruction of the marriage. Our relationship with God is no different.

Throughout Scripture, God never challenges whether doubt should exist. It is the one point of unity between us and God—the recognition that we struggle with faith, belief, and trust. Where we differ from God is what we think should follow doubt. We think the burden rests on God to erase our doubt. God knows that the burden rests on us to continue to trust and wait on Him, even in our doubt.

Our programmed response to confusion is doubt, while the Psalms teach us to respond to confusion with faith. We think doubt demands an answer. God thinks doubt demands faith.

We look at doubt and think it needs an urgent resolution. God looks at doubt and thinks we need patience and endurance.

It could be said that when we think doubt is the problem between us and God, the reality is that an absence of faith or trust might be the real problem.

CHOOSING REALITY

We need to learn to discipline ourselves to keep moving when we begin to be hung up by our doubts. Seeking healthy community is one way we do that. Another habit that can be helpful is the discipline of remembrance. We see an example of this in the story of Joshua. After the Israelites crossed the Jordan River, God instructed them to raise a memorial to remind them that He had delivered them: "'Let this be a sign among you, so that when your children ask later, saying, "What do these stones mean to you?" then you shall say to them, "Because the waters of the Jordan were cut off before the ark of the covenant of the LORD; when it crossed the Jordan, the waters of the Jordan were cut off"'" (Joshua 4:6–7 NASB).

Remembering the goodness of God can be difficult in the midst of challenging circumstances. Think back to the last time you were sick for longer than five days. When you've been sick for a week or more, it becomes difficult to remember what it feels like to be well. Sickness becomes your reality.

In a similar way doubt, pain, and frustration can easily become our reality. In the midst of losing a house, it can be difficult to remember all the cherished memories you have been blessed with there. In fact, your cherished memories might even contribute to your pain, because you realize that part of your life is ending.

The old phrase "count your blessings" might be trite, but it's apt. The discipline of remembrance is synonymous with the discipline of praise. I'm not saying we should praise God inauthentically by praying prayers we don't mean or singing songs we can't feel. But there is something powerful about disciplining ourselves to remember God's blessings and reminding ourselves of times when we've felt His presence and goodness.

Seven different times in the book of Deuteronomy God commands the Israelites to remember what He has done for them. The last time is in Deuteronomy 32:7: "Remember the days of old; consider the years of many generations; ask your father, and he will show you, your elders, and they will tell you" (ESV).

This verse also demonstrates that one of the ways to find our way back to faith during a season of doubt is to seek encouragement from our community.

When doubt becomes our reality, we completely lose sight of the big picture.

THE VANISHING BEES

In graduate school, a professor teaching philosophy of mind discussed a study with bees. This certain kind of bee would go and fetch pollen, bring it back, set it down, go and look inside the hive, where it was to take the pollen, and only then would it come back out, grab the pollen, and take it into the hive. The study was conducted to learn what would happen if someone *moved* the pollen while the bee was checking things out inside.

What happened was surprising. The bee would come back out and rearrange the pollen—and then go through the script again: look inside the hive, come back out, fetch the pollen, and take it into the hive. If the pollen was continually moved, the bee would be stuck in its programming and forever run through the motions of putting the pollen back in its place, going inside to look, coming out, finding the pollen moved, and then cycling back through the steps all over again.

The study was interesting from a philosophy of mind standpoint, as it spoke to the difference between a purely mechanistic animal and one with free will and consciousness: the bee couldn't transcend the change in its routine or the deviation from its expectations.

Often, when we are consumed by our doubt, we become like the bee that can't break out of the programmed pattern. We become hyper-focused on the single issue of which we can't let go, and cycle back to our mental tapes, our arguments of why something is not fair, why it is wrong, and how we cannot move on till things are put back aright.

What God is telling the Israelites in the Old Testament "remember" passages is to zoom out and consider the bigger picture. To see the whole context and be able to engage human consciousness and free will to move forward despite whatever the current circumstances might be.

The reality is that there are times of intense trauma or loss when we will be consumed by grief: the death of a child, natural disasters, school shootings, addiction, and so forth. It's not that we should slap a smile on our faces and pretend that nothing is wrong, but there is a powerful distinction between forgetting sorrow and remembering blessing.

We can embrace both.

Faith means holding these two things in tension: the goodness of God and our circumstances that scream out to the contrary. We can be honest with our doubts while leaning with trust into the arms of the God who holds us through our grief. That is the paradox of faith. It does not seem possible that a good God can allow bad things to happen to us. But if we can lean into His goodness and keep moving forward, we'll find Him on the other side of our doubts.

The story of our faith does not end when we doubt. Faith is not the absence of doubt; it is the remedy to doubt.

Doubt is only the beginning. It is in our doubt that we begin to truly find faith.

Only a faith that has been doubted can be confirmed.

Only a life that has been risked can be redeemed.

Only a God who has been trusted can prove Himself trustworthy.

For I am convinced that neither death nor life, neither angels nor demons, neither the present nor the future, nor any powers, neither height nor depth, nor anything else in all creation, will be able to separate us from the love of God that is in Christ Jesus our Lord.
—ROMANS 8:38–39

PERSONAL CALLING AND MISSION

It is as sharing in some faint degree in our Lord's High-Priestly action, bringing the needs of the world to the altar of God, and going forth from the altar of God bringing bread and wine to the needs of the world, that the Christian priest's life of prayer must be lived.[1]
—EVELYN UNDERHILL

Nothing good comes from Nazareth.

Most Bible readers—even the most dedicated ones—will likely be unfamiliar with the ancient city of Megiddo, which was situated in the northern hills of Israel and along the Jezreel Valley. But in the ancient world, this city held great strategic importance. In the words of Pharaoh Thutmose III (fifteenth century BC), "The capture of Megiddo is the capture of a thousand cities." This is because Megiddo sat along the *Via Maris*—or Way of the Sea—a major trade route situated along the Mediterranean Sea. This trade route was crossed over by other trade routes, which allowed people to travel between Africa, Europe, and Asia.

Whoever conquered Megiddo exercised significant control over trade in the known world, and whoever controlled trade thus controlled the economy, and whoever controlled the economy largely controlled the world.

Understandably, Megiddo became one of the most fought-over cities in the ancient world. Archaeologists have discovered at least twenty-six layers of civilization there. It is nicknamed the "City of Kings" because of the number of kings who conquered and ruled it. One of those kings was King Solomon, who refortified the city during his reign in the tenth century BC (1 Kings 9:15).

Just eleven miles across the Jezreel Valley and within eyesight from Megiddo is another city. Unlike Megiddo, however, this city today is one of the most familiar in the world: Nazareth—the boyhood town of Jesus.

But in the ancient world, Nazareth was not a place kings fought over, let alone talked about. When people sat around their campfires in Nazareth, they would have told stories about the kings who conquered and the warriors who fought over Megiddo. They did not tell stories about protagonists from Nazareth. There were none to tell.

Nazareth at the time of Jesus would have had only between four hundred and two thousand people. It wasn't mentioned in Jewish literature until the third century AD.

No wonder Nathanael was so dumbfounded when Philip told him that Jesus *of Nazareth* was the promised Messiah. "Nazareth! Can anything good come from there?" he asked (John 1:45–46). *The King of kings and the Lord of lords is not supposed to hail from Nazareth, is He?*

Sometimes the people God uses aren't the ones we see as most important. They don't come from where we expect, and they may not look significant.

The paradox of Nazareth is one more reminder of the paradox of Jesus, one more reminder of the paradox of the heavenly kingdom juxtaposed with the kingdoms of this world.

God's ways flip the ways of our culture upside down.

SELF-DECEPTION

At the center of the idea of "God's will for my life" lies a subtle self-deception that "life is really about me." We all like to think God's will for our individual lives is to write us into the story as the central character.

Whether we're aware of it or not, we carry with us a subtle sense in our pursuit of God or in our prayers, that at any moment we will break out of the fog or the challenges of life and enter into a season where it is all about us. Where God's plan has us in the driver's seat. Where we are each the most important person in the world. Where everyone else will recognize our extreme importance.

And self-righteousness always has its roots in self-centeredness.

With an inflated sense of our own importance, we tend to approach God as if He is eager to write us in as the central character in His drama—as Hamlet in the school play. The sin and selfishness in all of us is that we want to be the center of the universe. We see ourselves at the center of everything (and all things bending to meet our desires). It is subtle, and it can hide behind good intentions. The absurdity is the obvious fact that not everyone in the school play can be Hamlet. There is only one Hamlet, and everyone else, to some degree, is the supporting cast.

Nothing illustrates the false illusion of worldly power and centrality we have more than Jesus of Nazareth.

We want to write God into our story; but God prefers writing us into His.

Our flawed perspective shows itself in many ways. One of the most common phrases we hear in talks about suffering is, "God wants to build character, not comfort." It's one of those Christian sayings that you nod along with before you even finish hearing because it sounds so obviously spiritual. But the idea that suffering exists to bring character rather than comfort is flawed, as it still articulates a self-centered way of understanding the reality of daily life. Even the suffering and resultant character is ultimately focused on me and about me. I'm still the hero of the story, and the suffering only makes sense if it is to help me grow.

Self-deception has two related opposites, and both are essential to our becoming mature, to our becoming all that God intends us to be. And whereas making everything—even character-building—all about ourselves comes very easily to all of us, humility and teachability come only with difficulty and submission. T. S. Eliot wrote, "Humility is the most difficult of all virtues to achieve; nothing dies harder than the desire to think well of oneself."[2]

And related to the issues of humility and teachability is the issue of accurate self-assessment. According to G. K. Chesterton, "What embitters the world is not excess of criticism, but absence of self-criticism."[3]

Perhaps even more apt is Pascal's observation:

> It is no doubt an evil to be full of faults, but it is a still greater evil to be full of them and unwilling to recognize them, since this entails the further evil of deliberate self-delusion. We do not want others to deceive us; we do not think it right for them to want us to esteem them more than they deserve; it is therefore not right either that we should deceive them and want them to esteem us more than we deserve.[4]

Saint Augustine described the process as he experienced it back in the fourth century: "O Lord, you were turning me around to look at myself. For I had placed myself behind my own back, refusing to see myself. You were setting me before my own eyes so that I could see how sordid I was, how deformed and squalid, how tainted with ulcers and sores. I saw it all and stood aghast, but there was no place where I could escape from myself."[5]

This process isn't easy—it can be incredibly difficult, and messy. But it is critical. When we see ourselves for what we really are, the picture can be bleak and humbling. Becoming aware of our own pride and our own selfishness is the first step in becoming teachable enough to begin the process of renouncing some of our commitment to self.

Instead of asking what God's will is *for* my life, I should be asking how I can serve God's will *with* my life.

This subtle deception, thinking I'm talking about God's will when in fact I am really most concerned with myself, is why we're always looking for that dynamic, amazing plan God must have for our lives. It is why we have such a hard time with day-to-day faithful, righteous, and just living as a manifestation of God's will for how we should live.

This challenge is an enormous reality in a consumeristic society. Nearly everything reinforces the commitment to and primacy of self. Our culture does a better job of raising up consumers than instilling compassion. Both as a society and as individuals, we tend to focus much more on human rights than on human responsibilities. We see ourselves more often as the victims of society than as shapers of circumstance and members of society.

God doesn't promise that all will play the central character, or that we'll get to be the Moses, David, Rebekah, or Paul. What God does promise, however, is that He will love all, lead all, meet us all, and provide the guidance and wisdom needed through the Holy Spirit to find, rest in, and follow His leading in our lives.

But we still have questions. We still want guidance.

One of the most human of all questions is, "Why am I here?" It seeks to understand the role we play in the universe and extends to what we do and how we make life decisions on a daily basis.

And what about God's calling for my life? What is my purpose, and how does God want me to use my gifts?

Our heads spin with these questions and countless others every day. We recognize the significance of these governing questions and the decisions that follow them.

Much of life is governed by major decisions that affect all our other decisions and options. Where we go to school, whom we marry, and what profession we choose all affect virtually every other aspect of our lives. Unlike where I eat for lunch today, these bigger decisions affect everything downstream. So, understanding our purpose and making good decisions to higher-order questions is incredibly important.

GOD'S WILL FOR OUR LIFE

Though there are several biblical principles to help us define direction and chart our course in life as believers, the reality that God shows us in Scripture is that personal calling and mission are often best understood looking backward, rather than peering into the future.

Though life is messy and it is impossible to have perfect insight about the future, in Christ we can find hope that provides sufficient grounding for daily life. We must balance our desire for specific direction with an ability to be at peace in our current situation and the leading God has for us today.

Somewhere along the line, as Christians, we are led to believe that there is a very clear map of God's will for our lives, one that would make wisdom, prayer, and wise counsel from friends unnecessary because we would have such a clear understanding that all those things become irrelevant.

As the verses below illustrate, God's will is a broad concept, having to do with our minds and the entirety of our lives, rather than specific steps.

> Do not conform to the pattern of this world, but be transformed by the renewing of your mind. Then you will be able to test and approve what God's will is—his good, pleasing and perfect will. (Romans 12:2)

> For it is God's will that by doing good you should silence the ignorant talk of foolish people. (1 Peter 2:15)

> As a result, they do not live the rest of their earthly lives for evil human desires, but rather for the will of God. (1 Peter 4:2)

Believing this false ideal—that simply discerning the correct next step in life equates to walking in God's will—has become for Christians one of the most rampant and destructive impediments to our maturity and spiritual growth.

God's will in my life may not be so much about what college I attend, or a "mission impossible"–type message delivered to me about how I'm going to save the world before it self-destructs. Rather, it can often be more about *how* I live my life than the specifics of *what* I do.

The question isn't simply what will make me happy, but the more complex one of what is good, true, and beautiful, and what promises has God made that I can have peace in?

GOD WILL

It is a pretty powerful thing to see or hear God say, "I will." There are probably no stronger, more comforting, or more final words in life than when the sovereign God says, "I will."

I had a professor, Jerry Root, who once said that we can have sure words, but God gets last words.

There is no stronger last word in Scripture than when God declares, "I will."

These declarations are present throughout Scripture (note the added emphasis in all of the following passages). In Genesis, God said, "*I will* make you into a great nation, and *I will* bless you; *I will* make your name great" (12:2), and later, "I am with you and *will* watch over you wherever you go, and *I will* bring you back to this land. *I will not* leave you until I have done what I have promised" (28:15).

In Exodus He told His people, "I am the LORD, and *I will* bring you out from under the yoke of the Egyptians. *I will* free you from being slaves to them, and *I will* redeem you" (6:6). He continued, "*I will* establish your borders. . . . *I will* give into your hands the people who live in the land" (23:31).

He told Joshua, "Today *I will* begin to exalt you in the eyes of all Israel" (Joshua 3:7), and through the prophet Jeremiah He said, "See, *I will* defend your cause and avenge you" (Jeremiah 51:36).

Jesus used these strong words in Mark 14:58, "*I will* destroy this temple made with human hands and in three days *[I] will* build another, not made with hands." And in John 2:19 Jesus answered His enemies, "Destroy this temple, and *I will* raise it again in three days."

God's promises are backed by the declaration of His power and His intention to act. In everything, we can trust Him and rely on His power at work in the world and in our lives.

WHAT IS GOD'S PLAN FOR MY LIFE?

We may not all be the main character or have a dramatic calling, but some people will. And even if we don't, God cares about us deeply and has something for us as part of His glorious plan. Ephesians 1:11–12 says, "In him we were also chosen, having been predestined according to the plan of him who works out everything in conformity with the purpose of his will, in order that we, who were the first to put our hope in Christ, might be for the praise of his glory."

So how do we find our path? How do we surface the answer to our questions regarding God's will without succumbing to the idea that God has seven billion wills, one for every person? Could it be that God's singular will is big enough to fit seven billion people?

God often answers the bigger questions through a series of smaller questions and actions. There are a few principles along these lines I find useful when trying to discern where God is leading.

1. DO WHAT YOU ALREADY KNOW

The Bible is full of wisdom about godly living and God's will for us to become more like Him, to glorify Him, and to love others. Here is where we should start: with obedience to God and with faithfulness in our daily lives and relationships.

As Paul told the Christians in Thessalonica, "you do love all of God's family throughout Macedonia. Yet we urge you, brothers and sisters, to do so more and more, and to make it your ambition to lead a quiet life: You should mind your own business and work with your hands, just as we told you, so that your daily life may win the respect of outsiders and so that you will not be dependent on anybody" (1 Thessalonians 4:10–12).

Rather than acting on what we know, we Christians seem to spend a disproportionate amount of our time and energy trying to figure out the 10 percent of God's will that is mysterious. We are enamored with the part that seems exciting, engaging, and adventurous, and somewhat bored by doing the 90 percent that we already do know—the obvious, the cliché, the morally obligatory ways of living sacrificially with good character and faithfulness.

2. FIND GOD IN SOLITUDE

Nothing centers us more quickly than removing ourselves from daily routines and spending time in solitude with God.

The word *solitude* comes from the Latin word *solitudo*, meaning "loneliness," which has the root *solus*, meaning "alone." It's a subject we don't often talk about or think about.

When we think of what Jesus taught the disciples about prayer, we tend to reflect on the words. What we miss is the posture or position of prayer that they witnessed when they saw Him regularly spend lonely nights on mountaintops. It's as important as the words He said and the prayer He recited to them.

Arguably, Jesus' primary teaching on prayer was His personal example, which was so often set in the context of solitude.

Solitude is about being alone with God. We never hear God's plans for our lives more clearly than in solitude.

3. LEARN TO SEEK GUIDANCE RATHER THAN FINAL PLANS

Sometimes the more relevant prayer is not, "God, what is Your specific will for my life?" but, "God, help me understand what decisions to make today, what endeavors to undertake, what people to pursue, and which goals to set."

We have a class at Kilns College called Personal Calling and Mission. The goal of the class is to move students who are originally looking for a definitive, specific calling to having an understanding of prayer and a theology of seeking guidance. We want to create students mature enough to confidently and excitedly seek and follow God's leading in their lives on a daily basis.

Faith is not only a choice in the moment, but a commitment into the future. We don't always need to see where the road leads; we simply need the faithfulness and commitment to take the next few steps in front of us.

4. UNDERSTAND YOUR PASSIONS

I once heard the phrase, "Your misery is your ministry." It simply means that if something drives you crazy, then maybe you should do something about it. If you're the person always critiquing worship, maybe you should be involved in worship ministry. If you're really concerned about how children are taught, maybe you should be involved in children's ministries. If it frustrates you how homeless people are treated or ignored, maybe you should try to be more involved in social work and outreach.

In short, what really bugs you at a deep, spiritual level creates a lot of energy, focus, and passion for effecting change.

Our passions come from God, our experiences, and what we're good at—and they are often obvious places to start.

GOOD FROM NAZARETH?

"Can anything good come out of Nazareth?"

It was not the place of prominence, yet it is where God birthed His vision for salvation. Nobody could have foreseen it, but in many ways, looking back, it's consistent with all the other parts of God's saving work. God seems to always be about turning the categories of this world on their heads. Jesus was the picture of the insider becoming the outsider. He showed us the importance of the one with power surrendering it for the benefit of others.

Jesus is not the Hollywood hero, unless the Hollywood hero—taking his lead from the gospel narrative—patterns its plot after Him.

Part of faith is trusting that your calling, as well as your steps, may remain a mystery. Life is lived forward, but understood backward. What we can bank on is that when we surrender our plans to God, we'll find that we are successful at serving God.

Our personal calling and mission in life is often confusing. Paul wasn't so sure of his calling at the front end of his ministry. John the Baptist knew his calling from the beginning, but later suffered a crisis of doubt. Moses was certain that he had lost his calling. There's no formula or universal pattern for calling in the Christian life. What we are promised is that God is faithful, that He honors those who serve Him, and that we have been given the Holy Spirit specifically so we will have the guidance, leading, and input in our lives to faithfully and confidently continue forward.

In fact, faithfulness is often the best gateway to our calling or path in life.

Kierkegaard is said to have written, "To dare is to lose one's footing momentarily. Not to dare is to lose oneself." Pursuing your calling or ministry as a Christian is a big risk. It's hazarding your own life with the belief that somehow, there is no life apart from it.

Our idea of God's bigness, and the bigness of His plans, needs to grow. We get to join God in His work in the world. We are included, not out of necessity, but because of the relational nature of God and His plan that, not only would He be righteous, holy, and loving, but that His creation would be so as well.

What is God's will for your life? Simple. It is that you live out *His* will for the world. That you bring goodness, truth, and beauty to the world.

Christianity doesn't serve me; I serve the cause of Christ.

As Jesus went on from there, he saw a man named
Matthew sitting at the tax collector's booth. "Follow me,"
he told him, and Matthew got up and followed him.
—MATTHEW 9:9

LOVE IS NEVER WRONG

Faith makes all things possible . . . love makes all things easy.[1]
—D. L. Moody

We recently had the chance to take our four daughters to a few of the national parks in the West. The kids were so excited, so we decided to buy the lengthy Ken Burns documentary detailing the history of the national parks—a long story full of drama, politics, and its fair share of wild characters.

The first park to be established was Yosemite, which was originally given to the state of California to manage. Therefore, the second park—Yellowstone—was the first true national park. Yellowstone is in what at that time was still the Wyoming Territory (not yet a state), so it had to be managed by the federal government.

The creation of the National Park System began during the Theodore Roosevelt era. Roosevelt was an intellectual, an imposing political strategist, and because of his many early experiences out west, a lover of America's natural wonders. He visited the West often and, at times, left his travel companions to go off into the wild alone or with the likes of naturalist John Muir.

In 1906, Congress passed a bill giving the president authority to designate national monuments, although declaring a national park remained a congressional right. This bill was intended to streamline the process by which the president could protect important places—archaeological ruins or other points of national interest. Roosevelt was not a timid man and pushed the boundaries of this new authority by naming dozens of national monuments. He even named the Grand Canyon, which covered more than 1.2 million acres and whose designation as a national park had faced stiff opposition from Congress, a national monument.[2]

The story goes that Teddy Roosevelt once asked, "Is there any law that prevents me declaring Pelican Island a National Bird Sanctuary?" He paused only briefly and then said, "Very well, then," reached for his pen, and said, "I do declare it."[3]

When conviction and authority intersect, it's easy to act.

BACK TO BASICS

Roosevelt's confidence and passion about natural resources might illuminate the type of confidence and passion we should have as Christians, living in a valuable creation with valuable people.

In one sense, this chapter is something you've probably heard since the day you became a Christian, or maybe even before that:

- God is love.
- Forgiveness matters.
- Be humble.
- Love your enemies.
- Do good.
- Pray.

It sounds familiar but I think there's a subtle deception that we live with: learning about God is always going to be new and exciting, a constant exploration of uncharted territory. We are always on the hunt for the next profound revelation.

Sometimes modern Christianity encourages us to derive Christian principles, action steps, and application maxims from every lesson and every sermon. The danger is that where Jesus really only offered one command—to love—we populate the heavens with *shoulds* and *oughts*.

Similarly, in our Christian walk we face many ups and downs that are full of emotion. God gives us emotions—and like anything, they can either help or hurt. The downside of emotion is when it makes following God's will more difficult. But if I can rest on a few simple principles and stay focused there, then I can stand on something—even if I don't feel it or understand why I'm doing it in a given situation.

The solution to learning how to live for Christ isn't more insight or more feeling, but more commitment. It isn't about knowing more, but obeying more. In the midst of doubt, messiness, and confusion, rather than trying to uncover deep mysteries, we can always return to what we know already—like a football team that goes "back to the basics."

It can actually be simple.

Christianity isn't exciting because it's new or novel or because there's some new secret we're going to uncover. It is exciting because it leads us continually back into the heart of what it means to be human and made in the image of God.

NEVER WRONG

Have you ever felt that sometimes religion is less like a way of life, and more like a system of behavior modification? That something is broken in the way we present Christianity? That there are too many rules for anyone to follow perfectly?

For those who truly care about love and justice, one of the most disappointing experiences in religion is when it becomes a man-made system of conformity and standardization that we use to judge each other.

Conform yourself to the right behaviors, at least externally, and you can pass as being religious, spiritual, or good. Many times the focus is on the things we shouldn't do. Such a legalistic focus can easily lend itself to judgment, guilt, and a straitlaced, duty-bound faith. Meanwhile, all the attention is focused on measuring ourselves by who has been *less bad*, rather than actively seeking to reflect the grace and love of Christ. In the life of faith it can be counterproductive to guard our moral status and make perfect righteousness our goal.

Certainly this isn't the life to which God has called us.

What would happen if we flipped the system around? What if religion was primarily focused on doing the things that are *never* wrong, rather than avoiding the things that are *always* wrong? In fact, isn't pursuing religious perfection the very thing that sometimes keeps us from pursuing justice?

As Jesus admonished the religious leaders, "Woe to you, teachers of the law and Pharisees, you hypocrites! You give a tenth of your spices—mint, dill and cumin. But you have neglected the more important matters of the law—justice, mercy and faithfulness. You should have practiced the latter, without neglecting the former" (Matthew 23:23).

Christ *has* given us permission to flip things upside down. Like Roosevelt, we have authority. We have the mandate. Is there any law that prevents us from doing things that are never wrong?

Instead of managing behavior, maybe we should be simply living rightly. The surest way to become just and righteous is to live justly and righteously.

As I've reflected on this idea, I keep returning to several themes of behaviors in this positive vein. Here are five things in Scripture that I believe are never wrong:

HUMILITY

First Peter 5:5 says, "God opposes the proud but shows favor to the humble." Ephesians 4:2 says, "Be completely humble and gentle." And we're familiar with Jesus' words in Matthew 20:16, "The last will be first, and the first will be last." These verses convey that there is never a time when authentic humility is frowned on by God or a bad strategy for life. It is always a good thing, and never wrong, to be humble. Saint Augustine put it this way: "Humility is the foundation of all the other virtues hence, in the soul in which this virtue does not yet exist there cannot be any other virtue except in mere appearance."[4]

REPENTANCE

First John 1:9 says, "If we confess our sins, he is faithful"; Isaiah 30:15 says, "In repentance and rest is your salvation"; and in Matthew 18:22, Jesus told Peter to forgive his brother "not seven times, but seventy-seven times." In Scripture, confessing sins and repenting—saying you're sorry—is always virtuous and a healthy part of maintaining and restoring relationship with God and others. Do you want to move your life forward today? Think of somebody you can forgive, and forgive that person. Think of something for which you need to apologize, and do so. When it comes to creating a just world, one of the best things we can do is to say, "I'm sorry." It's also often the hardest response, but repentance is never wrong.

FAITH

Hebrews 11:6 says, "Without faith it is impossible to please God." We also sense Jesus' discouragement with His followers throughout the book of Matthew when He says, "O you of little faith" (for example, 6:30; 14:31 ESV). God desires to nurture in us and draw out of us a greater faith, a stronger reliance upon Him, and a readier trust in His promises that we would end each day with greater faith than when we began that day. Faith is always good and never wrong.

PRAYER

Paul tells us in 1 Thessalonians 5:17 to "pray continually." And the 150 psalms, or songs of prayer, in the middle of Scripture make it very clear to us that it's always appropriate to pray. There's never a time when turning our eyes and tuning our ears to God falls outside the bounds of what we should be doing in that moment. Prayer is never wrong.

THE GREATEST OF THESE IS LOVE

But probably more important than all these others is the idea that *love* is never wrong. In Galatians 5:22–23, love is listed as the first of many attributes that make up the fruits of the Spirit. These verses close by saying, "Against such things there is no law." This means that there is never a time when love or these other virtues are legislated against. Therefore, there is never a time when love is wrong.

Jesus commands us to love, and, in his famous passage on love in 1 Corinthians 13, Paul wrote, "Love is patient, love is kind. It does not envy, it does not boast, it is not proud" (v. 4). In verse 8, he declared, "Love never fails." Love is both a sanction and an imperative. It is a sanction in that it is always good, and it is an imperative in that we should always do it.

There is no law, no legislation, no case against love. It is never wrong. We can, of course, do foolish and even very harmful things from a *motivation* of love (as the classic dictum observes, "the road to hell is paved with good intentions"), but that is a separate issue for another time.[5] Biblical and sacrificial love is not only fully sanctioned, but mandated.

Jesus' strongest commands are more focused on what to *do* rather than what *not* to do. And this loving others is a command woven throughout all of Scripture.

We find this command in Leviticus 19:18: "Love your neighbor as yourself." Jesus quoted Deuteronomy 6:5 and this verse and then expostulated on them: "'Love the Lord your God with all your heart and with all your soul and with all your mind.' This is the first and greatest commandment. And the second is like it: 'Love your neighbor as yourself.' All the Law and the Prophets hang on these two commandments'" (Matthew 22:37–40).

Writing to the church at Galatia, Paul added, "You, my brothers, were called to be free. But do not use your freedom to indulge the sinful nature; rather, serve one another in love. The entire law is summed up in a single command: 'Love your neighbor as yourself'" (Galations 5:13–14).

One of the best ways to follow Jesus and develop authentic spirituality is to start each day with a mental framework of love. With this mind-set, we ask, "Who am I going to bless? Who could I encourage?" And, motivated by love, "What offense can I overlook?"

Choosing love will slowly begin to weed sin out of our behavior patterns. Jesus saw the avoidance of sin as a by-product of choosing love. We are commanded to love, and every failure to love is a sin. The one who loves is the one who is not sinning.

One of the early church leaders, Augustine, in his commentary on the book of 1 John, summed up the principle by simply stating, "Love and do as you please."[6] If our hearts are oriented toward the love of God and others, then all that follows will sort itself out.

Mother Teresa said it this way: "I have found the paradox, that if you love until it hurts, there can be no more hurt, only more love."

If love comes with a sanction and an imperative, then there is never a time when it is wrong and never a time when it can be ignored. It's something we can be sure of and something we can always return to.

Love is.

Love does.

Love holds.

Love believes.

Love suffers.

Love gives.

And love is never wrong.

LOVE AS SACRAMENT

In my first book, *Pursuing Justice*, I included a chapter called "Love as Sacrament." In it I tried to show the curious, unfortunate, and rather significant shift in our culture's understanding of the word *love*. Love, culturally speaking, is usually meant to denote the intensity of our wants, wishes, or desires. If we long for something, that must mean we love it. If we really want something, we say we really love it. If we have an intense desire for it, we must love, love, LOVE it!

When we define love in terms of desire or wants, what we're in effect doing is replacing love's deep meaning with the definition of lust—*intense want or desire*. It is shocking that we've inadvertently turned *love* into a synonym for *lust*.

This is radically different from the way Jesus measured love. In John 15, He said that love has no greater expression than laying one's life down for a brother or sister (v. 13). Sacrifice, with its ultimate expression in giving up one's life for another, is at the heart of love. Whereas for our culture the metric is desire, for Jesus the metric of love is sacrifice and service.

The word *sacrifice* shares the same root as the word *sacrament*, which has for us a very spiritual and religious connotation. And the commonality of these two words can be seen in a well-known event in Jesus' ministry. As He sat with His disciples the night before He gave His life as a *sacrifice*, Jesus took and passed the bread and wine—in what Christians called the *sacrament* of communion, or the Lord's Supper—and said, "This is My blood. This is My body, broken for you." What Jesus was literally saying to His disciples that night as He held out the wine and the bread was, "Here is the full measure of My love."

As we participate in the sacraments of communion, marriage, or baptism, we are entering into, remembering, and hopefully calling to mind the definition of love. It's a great irony that individuals can often partake of the sacraments of Jesus, thinking only of the religious benefits for themselves, while missing completely the fact that they are entering into love-saturated symbolism.

As we begin to wrap our minds fully around Jesus' understanding of and the scriptural mandates for love, we won't be able to participate in the sacraments or in any religious rituals without coming away marked and shaped by the love of God in Christ and compelled to reflect the same love for humanity.

SIMPLY LOVE

In Romans 13:8, Paul stated, "Let no debt remain outstanding, except the continuing debt to love one another, for he who loves his fellow man has fulfilled the law."

Love fulfills the law.

Grace wins over legalism.

Sadly, however, there is a long history of trading the positive call of love into a set of religious rules, a set of sins to avoid, or a form of behavior management that keeps us looking externally pure and righteous. Such a negative focus is a lot like playing defense with no thought to offense.

Jesus, by contrast, spent a lot of time talking about what we should be doing—the kinds of things that are always right and never wrong.

It's a lot like learning to ride a bike. Forward momentum is a much more powerful balancing force than sitting on a bike, trying to keep it from tipping. The wise father will direct his child's focus toward building forward momentum, knowing that balance, and avoiding falling to the left or the right, is largely resolved through the bike's momentum. Likewise, Christ's mandates and the call to follow Him all speak to a momentum in the life of the believer that handles much of errant behavior through positive focus and pursuit.

We have the authority and the mandate to run forward—to write new national monuments into existence.

If you want to walk forward with confidence, if you want to put down sure steps, find the things that are never wrong, always right, and do those things—even in times of doubt and uncertainty.

I have tried to raise my daughters not to be afraid of making mistakes. Rather, my hope for them is that they would be excited about experimenting and trying and testing. We try to let them paint, bake, sing, create, and serve without worrying whether they have it exactly right or perfect.

I want my daughters to be confident. To know that they can do some good.

Jesus says childlike faith is our best template, which means faith isn't beyond us. We can do this. We can get excited about being wholeheartedly, confidently engaged in the aspects of faith that are never wrong.

Faith doesn't require a stratospheric IQ, encyclopedic knowledge, a PhD, good looks, exceptional talent, or any other worldly measure of value or credibility. Faith requires obedience.

Who has been the most encouraging person in your faith walk? The person who gave you a huge list of dos and don'ts probably didn't have the greatest influence on you. It was probably the person who most made you feel you could succeed.

God has told us, as a dad tells his kids, "Go out in the world." Jesus said in Matthew 5:14, "You are the light of the world." There's an exciting assumption buried in what Jesus was saying: What God has called us to do is something He's made possible for us to do. We can do it. We have the mandate and the authority.

You have gifts, talents, and the ability to love. Be empowered. Be encouraged. The God who calls us to love has given us the capacity to love.

> For the LORD is good and his love endures forever; his
> faithfulness continues through all generations.
> —PSALM 100:5

COMPLEXITY AND THE LIMITS OF HUMAN UNDERSTANDING

It is the duty of the human understanding to understand that there are things which it cannot understand, and what those things are. Human understanding has vulgarly occupied itself with nothing but understanding, but if it would only take the trouble to understand itself at the same time it would simply have to posit the paradox.[1]
—Søren Kierkegaard

Immanuel Kant once reportedly said, "Science is organized knowledge. Wisdom is organized life." If anything, it has become more and more difficult since the time of Kant and Lady Wisdom to keep up with the complexities of our rapidly changing world.[2]

One of Kant's contemporaries, Johann Georg Heinzmann, a German publisher in the 1700s, was distressed by the number of books being printed. He even wrote an essay about it—*Appeal to My Nation: On the Plague of German Books*—in which he said, "No nation has printed so much as the

Germans."[3] Another German, jurist and philosopher Christian Thomasius, called the proliferation of books an "epidemic disease."[4]

Even ancient scholars were concerned about too much study and reading. Seneca, the Roman philosopher who said, "Leisure without books is death,"[5] also said, "The abundance of books is distraction."[6] As we'll see later, thousands of years before him, King Solomon wrote in Ecclesiastes about being wearied by too much study (12:12).

In our world, digital information is exploding exponentially, and technology is making communication easier and faster every year. We are directly affected by the realities of information overload.

Here are some statistics that bear that out:

- The equivalent of five hundred years of video are watched on Facebook every day.[7]
- One hundred hours of video are uploaded to YouTube every minute—that's a daily amount of more than sixteen years.[8]
- The average mobile phone user checks his or her phone 150 times a day.[9]
- There was a ninefold increase in the amount of digital information created and shared in the last five years.[10]
- The English version of *Wikipedia* alone grows at a rate of seven hundred articles per day.[11]

The availability of information and opportunity is skyrocketing.

Reading statistics of the speed of information and the pace of modern American life is in stark contrast to the pace and leisure experts in the 1960s thought technological advancement would bring by the end of the twentieth century where they projected Americans "could have either a twenty-two-hour work week, a six-month work year, or a standard retirement age of thirty-eight."[12]

In Scripture, it seems, the expectations for simplicity are different from what we find now. But those days are gone, and the expectations we place on ourselves and each other seem to be multiplying. Quickly.

Now, in the age of digital media, globalization, and the Internet, it appears the limits of knowledge and understanding are infinite. We can literally read about any event, any place, any person, and any topic we want. We can learn anything and everything no matter how obscure or irrelevant the topic. There are millions of books to read, movies to watch, and places to visit. Our culture produces a torrent of information consuming our time, energy, attention, and imagination.

We have loads of information; but do we have transformation?

Though learning, traveling, and understanding are all good things, is there a saturation point? Is there a point where the pressure to do and see everything becomes unhealthy? How do we know when to stop, take a step back, and let go of our hunger for more? When we can always do more, it requires trust to stop and not do any more. When we can always fight to get ahead, it requires faith to sit at the Lord's feet. As many teachers remind: we're human beings, not human doings.

What are the effects of these influences on our faith? How are we supposed to cling to faith in the midst of such a turbulent era?

The truth is, we're not the first Christians to experience the crisis of faith in the midst of stressful living. Imagine trying to cling to faith in medieval Europe during the bubonic plague, or working under slave conditions in antiquity. What if you were homeless in the hills of Palestine, hounded by religious leaders, knowing you might at any moment be put to death by a foreign power—would faith be any easier?

There is a paradox in that God calls us to immerse ourselves in redemptive engagement in this world, but to do so we must create Sabbath space from the world to rest from the barrage of information.

EVERYTHING IS DIFFERENT

Change is one of our culture's few constants. If our era will be defined by anything, it will be defined by the sweeping changes that have occurred. The Internet and media are rapidly reshaping the way we do everything: shop, interact, meet, and share news.

An example of the incredible changes that have taken place over the last 150 years can be seen in the life of Igor Stravinsky. Stravinsky was one of the most influential composers of the twentieth century. If you've seen either of Disney's *Fantasia* movies, you have heard his music.[13]

He was born in Russia in 1882, when the modern automobile was non-existent, and died in 1971, two years after the crew of the *Apollo 11* mission *walked on the moon*. Can you imagine growing up in a world without cars, then being barraged with earth-shattering revolutions the rest of your life: electric light, human flight, two world wars, assembly lines and mass production, the telephone, television, plastic, radio, rocket science, space travel, and moon walks?

Stravinsky responded to all this change by becoming a musical chameleon, constantly adapting and shifting his style throughout his life. In his autobiography he wrote, "Music is the sole domain in which man realizes the present."[14]

Now, more than forty years after his death, change continues to accelerate rather than slow down. Electronics, the Internet, globalization, and media are transforming the world at breakneck speed. In the midst of it all, we can have a difficult time knowing what to hang on to and what to let go.

CHASING AFTER THE WIND

When we find ourselves surrounded by rapid change, the natural reaction is to try to keep up. The Internet and social media make it seem possible—with the ease of a touch, we can easily listen to all the latest music, watch all the latest videos, and read breaking news tweeted live from where it's happening.

As a result, the techno-savvy culture is in a constant state of distraction. Eventually we find ourselves drowning in an ocean of distraction—a riptide of texts, e-mail alerts, Facebook notifications, and advertisements is constantly surging at us, driving us out to sea and away from the serenity of life's fundamentals. We wonder how we got there and how we've lost the meaning of life.

Ironically, one day while working, I ran across a graphic representation of the potential cost of distraction in the American workplace. Here are some of the stats compiled from *Forbes* magazine, CNN, *Psychology Today*, and other sources:[15]

- Workers are interrupted every 10.5 minutes by social media notifications.
- It then takes 23 minutes for those employees to get back on task.
- That's $650 billion of work hours a year, which is more than seven times the amount of money lost due to smoking breaks and more than the combined value of Google and Chevron.

Distraction is a real phenomenon, and it is causing real problems.

But isn't the ability to multitask an asset? Aren't there benefits to being able to simultaneously process a lot of information from various sources? Yes and no. Unfortunately, we rarely stop to consider the downsides. In a 2009 study conducted by late Stanford professor Clifford Nass, chronic multitaskers actually underperformed non-multitaskers in every cognitive test they were given. According to the study, multitaskers "have greater difficulty filtering out irrelevant stimuli from their environment . . . they are less likely to ignore irrelevant representations in memory . . . and they are less effective in suppressing the activation of irrelevant task sets."[16]

In other words, multitasking without discipline has the potential to reprogram us for distraction. Rather than developing the superpower of taking in more information at a time, some multitaskers are actually losing their ability to focus and filter out irrelevant information, making it harder for them to learn, get work done, and pay attention to what they are doing.

The danger with more and more information is that we can end up knowing less and less.

During the Renaissance and the height of the philosophy of humanism, there were some great thinkers, like Leonardo da Vinci, who believed a person could truly become an expert in multiple disciplines. Even so, these men, who mastered multiple languages, art forms, sciences, and philosophies, were not masters of *everything*.

Our modern interpretation of what it is to be a Renaissance man or woman has expanded to include mastery of all the arts and sciences, and the countless nuances of knowledge that we can google. Despite the fact that it is harder to be a modern-day Renaissance man or woman, some of us continue to operate as though it ought to be done. It's certainly a temptation for me as I try to wrap my mind around church ministry, education, justice, and how they all relate. Sometimes I feel pressure to read every book, watch every documentary, and visit every historic site I can.

FINDING YOUR RHYTHM

Is this raging drive to know and understand *everything* a biblical one? Not according to Ecclesiastes. Here are a couple of passages from Ecclesiastes about study and never-ending work:

> There was a man all alone;
>> he had neither son nor brother.
>> There was no end to his toil,
>> yet his eyes were not content with his wealth.
>> "For whom am I toiling," he asked,
>> "and why am I depriving myself of enjoyment?"
>> This too is meaningless—
>> a miserable business! (4:8)

> Of making many books there is no end, and much study wearies the body. (12:12)

Perhaps at this point you are recalling all the proverbs you have read about hard work and pursuing wisdom that sound like direct contradiction of the idea that "much study wearies the body." Such as this, also written by

Solomon:

> Let the wise hear and increase in learning,
>   and the one who understands obtain guidance,
>   to understand a proverb and a saying,
>   the words of the wise and their riddles.
>   The fear of the LORD is the beginning of knowledge;
>   fools despise wisdom and instruction. (Proverbs 1:5–7 ESV)

Is Solomon contradicting himself? Or is there a principle of rhythm here that we are missing? Let's look at the Sabbath command for some more perspective:

> Remember the Sabbath day, to keep it holy. Six days you shall labor, and do all your work, but the seventh day is a Sabbath to the LORD your God. (Exodus 20:8–10 ESV)

Look at the reasoning behind the command, given in verse 11: "For in six days the LORD made heaven and earth . . . and rested on the seventh day" (ESV). Today, we sometimes treat rest as if it is optional. Was the Sabbath a Hebraic law that only made sense for an agrarian culture? Was it only for the periods before the industrial explosion and later digital explosion?

Solomon was trying to explain in Ecclesiastes that enough is enough. He was presenting a principle of rhythm, rest, and trust in resolving the paradox, a gift given for God's people in any and all ages. Solomon assured us that God has designed us for rhythm, rest, trust, and relationship.

While God has always given provision for renewal and restoration for His people, culture tells us there's always something more we have to learn. It tangles us in systems that never end, like social media and the Internet.

The Sabbath hits the "reset" button. Through Sabbath, God reminds us we are made in His image and loved by Him. He realigns us to our calling and purpose in life, those things we can accomplish. He prescribes for us a calling that is attainable, and that isn't going to lead to depression, joylessness, and isolation. Such things are more characteristic of modern culture than of the kingdom of God.

CHOOSING OUR HEROES

Since Martin Luther, the heroes of the Protestant faith have often historically been academic theologians. What is frequently missed is the value that the Catholic tradition placed on simple saints, like monks and nuns. As a result, the text-based culture of Protestant churches spent tremendous energy trying to understand God, but slowly de-emphasized the importance of solitude and simply *being with* God.

Because we follow and emulate our heroes, we must choose them intentionally. If we choose academic theologians, there will be no end to our trying to understand God. The bigger question might be, where should we begin our journey with God?

The masters program at Kilns College seeks to redeem education. Though there is a wealth of good traditional schooling available, we also need places of study that are less about information gathering or vocational training and more about the flourishing of the human soul. There has to be an end to the complexity so the conversation on simplicity can emerge.

Though Brother Lawrence is a fairly famous name now, during his lifetime (c. 1614–1691) he was simply a monk at the Discalced Carmelite priory in Paris who worked in the kitchen and repaired sandals. In fact, he had such a lowly position because he lacked the education to become a cleric.[17] He has since become a powerful voice for simplicity and the joy of being in constant communion with God.

Lawrence penned: "Think about God as often as you can, day and night, in everything you do. He is always with you. Just as you would be rude if you deserted a friend who was visiting you, why would you be disrespectful of God by abandoning His presence?"[18]

Lately there has been a resurgence of people finding these Christian voices of peace and serenity, people learning that there's a Christian tradition of mindfulness, of being aware of the presence of God in the little things, and of stilling our souls to walk in faith moment by moment.

THE NEW LAW

Speaking of Christian voices, who doesn't keep adding more books to their "to-read" list? Everyone's stack keeps getting bigger and bigger, especially the stack of spiritual books. The pressure to consume more and more spiritual information keeps increasing.

We've made information the new Law, and nobody can obey it perfectly. Just as the Law of the Old Testament couldn't be satisfied, the goal of keeping up with the Information Age can't be satisfied, but to the extent that we attempt it, we're living under a new tyrant.

We feel as though we have to be able to defend the doctrine of the Trinity, to learn about the Gnostic gospels, to pick a side in the latest cultural controversy, and to read whatever is the latest Christian best seller.

God loves us for who we are. He has grace for us. We can put off reading that book. We can say no to that conference. We can skip watching that spoken-word video. We can just be children loved by a compassionate Father. And if you're a father or mother, you know the joy of simply being with and enjoying your children.

Do you want to please God? It's simple: just spend time with Him.

MORE GOD, LESS ADVICE

Sometimes we simply need more of God and less advice. Typically, if I am bothered by something, I go looking for more information about it. But if the problem *is* information, more information won't solve the problem or relieve the tension. Sometimes all the advice keeps us from simply taking a step forward and crying out to God.

At some psychological level, we're addicted to our approach to information, and it's hard to resist the temptation to try to subtract by continuing to add.

I toyed with the idea of titling the introduction "Why This Book Is Part of the Problem." In some ways I believe it is. More information is not the solution to an overload of information. Stepping out of the current is the answer.

Maybe that's why you're reading this book. Maybe the only thing you needed to get out of this book was the permission to close it. We need to find balance, not pile information onto existing mounds of information.

No doctor treats a cancer patient with more cancer. No psychologist treats anxiety with more stress. We need to stem the tide, not dump another stream of water into it.

ESCAPE

There is a *strong* biblical precedent of solitude and quiet as a requirement for being able to hear and understand God. Jesus exemplified this lifestyle: "Very early in the morning, while it was still dark, Jesus got up, left the house and went off to a solitary place, where he prayed" (Mark 1:35).

When we spend all our time trying to hear God, not in solitude, but through the cultural noise, the message can often be a little obscured or confusing.

Jesus says His yoke is easy and His burden is light. If His way constitutes a model for our lives, then we must be able to live into it. We *can* make our way to the eye of the hurricane, which is what it feels like to live closely with God in a chaotic world. Circumstances won't always change, but we can find a sense of peace in the presence of God.

There are the realities of God in the midst of confusion. We have to wrestle with them, because that's what the life of faith is going to mean. It is not simply that I hold a Christian creed, all the while being sucked into the riptide and pulled into the world with nothing to hold on to and no end to the drowning.

When we are reminded of the eternal part of our being, we can flip the table on our light and momentary obsessions. The ray of light in the complexity of the moment is that we are eternal creatures. We can stand outside of that complexity . . . again in paradox.

In the face of our hectic culture, there is no formula, no easy answer; but instead, there is the principle of rest and trust and waiting. There is the reality of God there, available, wanting to still my soul, and to lead me.

Rest is the cultural Dramamine we need to navigate our cultural landscape. And in order to navigate it, we're going to need to know what it looks like. The next chapter will tackle some of the most common pitfalls of the cultural landscape, and how we can seek out the proper alternatives.

"Come to me, all who labor and are heavy laden, and I will give you rest. Take my yoke upon you, and learn from me, for I am gentle and lowly in heart, and you will find rest for your souls. For my yoke is easy, and my burden is light."
—MATTHEW 11:28–30 ESV

CULTURAL LANDSCAPES

Wonder rather than doubt is the root of knowledge.[1]
—ABRAHAM JOSHUA HESCHEL

One of my favorite memories of reading to my kids has to do with C. S. Lewis's *The Voyage of the Dawn Treader*. The opening line in this book is one of my favorite openings of any book. It begins, "There was a boy called Eustace Clarence Scrubb, and he almost deserved it."[2]

Eustace, a cousin of the Pevensie children who are main characters throughout The Chronicles of Narnia, was a dull, un-imaginative and contentious child who had been schooled (in the negative sense of the word) by his parents to become such. Midway through the book on a deserted island, Eustace runs away and sees a large scaly creature crawling along in front of a cave.

Lewis, as the narrator, remarks to the reader, "Most of us know what we should expect to find in a dragon's lair, but, as I said before, Eustace had read only the wrong books."[3] I looked up from the book and asked, "What kind of creature is this, girls?" In near-perfect unison, they shouted: "IT'S A DRAGON!"

It was a bit of a setup, but I was so proud that my girls have read the *right* kind of books—fairy tales, fantasy, and imaginative fiction. Lewis, as a literary scholar and lover of mythology, always felt that imagination was important for the development of a whole person.

Lewis wasn't the only one who felt that imagination was important. A hundred years earlier, Charles Dickens penned his semiautobiographical novel *Hard Times*. In it, stony schoolmasters repress the imaginations of children and demand that they only learn facts and figures. One girl named Louisa Gradgrind gets caught saying the words "I wonder." Her father swiftly reproves her: "Louisa, never wonder!"[4]

I once worked with a children's director at a church who felt the same as Louisa's father—that imagination and wonder were suspect at best and dangerous at worst. She wanted only cold, hard biblical facts taught in her children's ministry, without anyone using or allowing imagination as part of the teaching process. No talking animals, no fairy tale illusions, and nothing fanciful.

Sound ridiculous? Of course it does. Jesus Himself used stories and parables to illustrate ethical and theological teaching, and He was talking to adults! We were created to love story, to learn from story, and to use our imaginations to teach, to learn, to live.

Story and art are often vehicles for depth. Even after we accept an idea intellectually, story can bring the idea alive emotionally and give us, in a way, a more direct or complete understanding of it. It allows us to see the way the idea works in "real life" and catch its details and nuance. Often, what looks like paradox as an abstract intellectual statement starts to make sense when we place it in the broader framework of the story.

Unfortunately, digging deep enough to develop complete understanding is something we often fail to do.

This problem is not limited to church culture; it can be found in the culture at large as well. It's one of the things that have concerned my wife and me as we have watched the arts drained from public education by many of the recent cutbacks and curriculum changes.

I think our culture can sometimes make us feel that we aren't really allowed to wonder. That reality is cold and hard, and that maturity requires a certain lack of wonder and imagination. That life is simple and apparent. But it's not.

A necessary part of living a life of faith in Christ is properly understanding the culture in which we live. This includes identifying those aspects of it that run counter to God's kingdom (or counter to being fully human), so that we may eschew them personally or engage them in battle for the sake of those in our spheres of influence.

This chapter is a brief look at aspects of our own cultural landscapes; it is, of course, not exhaustive, but meant to start us thinking intentionally about these issues.

FLATTENED IDEAS

Our cultural landscape surrounds us, influencing us through media, conversation, upbringing, language, and much more. This can encourage several unwitting mistakes, particularly if we let ourselves get too distracted by current cultural memes.

Theology is complex. Philosophy is complex. Science is complex. People are complex. There are details about you that I will never know that influence why you eat what you eat for dinner, what time you like to eat it, how you hold your utensils, what seat at the table you prefer, and what you think is appropriate to wear at the table. If I were to try to describe your idea of dinner without these nuances, I would fail in some way to describe the real you.

The same is true of God, of faith, of culture, and of life. To fully understand our context—and ourselves—we have to learn to delve deep. To take the time to learn, dialogue, process, and grow.

Ever heard a really silly "What would Jesus do?" question, like "Would Jesus be vegan?" Or "Would Jesus drive a minivan?"

Sometimes we cloud meaningful topics with meaningless ideas. Did you ever notice that chicken is never mentioned in the Old Testament? With all its rules about clean and unclean animals, pigeons, doves, quail, what to eat, when to eat, and how to eat, it says nothing about chicken.

The reason? Nobody ate chicken in the Middle East when the Old Testament was written. The ancestor of the modern chicken, the red jungle fowl, originated in India.[5] If we tried to interpret the Bible's silence about chicken as intentional or meaningful in any way, we would be missing the whole reason the silence is there.

The Old Testament was written within a particular cultural context, just like the New Testament. The details matter. Abraham, Moses, and David all existed within their own particular context. So did Jesus and Paul. So do you and I.

Picture the Roman Empire in your head. We each have a picture of the Roman Empire. If I asked you to describe it, you might imagine a picture of senators in togas, gladiator battles in a coliseum, or legions of armor-clad soldiers with red capes. But "Rome wasn't built in a day" is a cliché for a reason.

The real Roman Empire spanned eight hundred years of history and was as diverse as the entire known world. Romans didn't suddenly seize control of the entire known world with a fully established government.

The empire had a rise, a peak, and a fall, and the experience of both Romans and non-Romans was very different during each. It had different governmental structures and different leaders. It went through periods of peace and periods of intense military activity, both at home and abroad. It looked one way in southern Britain, another in Rome, and another in Palestine.

But we flatten eight hundred years of *global* history into one simple idea: the Roman Empire.

Seems like something is missing, right?

REINHOLD NIEBUHR

Reinhold Niebuhr was one of the most influential theologians of the twentieth century. In some ways he was the master of practical theology, or the process of taking the Bible and biblical principles and putting them into real life. In the original and best-known form of his famous "Serenity Prayer," Niebuhr prayed, "God, give us grace to accept with serenity the things that cannot be changed, courage to change the things that should be changed, and the wisdom to distinguish the one from the other."[6]

An early twentieth-century American, Niebuhr appeared in a suit and tie with a penetrating gaze and a hint of a smile on his life-worn, weary face. He believed that sin and the realities of the human condition were to be observed and confronted, not ignored. He lived out his life in the turbulent environments of early-twentieth-century Detroit and mid-century New York City. As a pastor during World War I, World War II, and the Vietnam War, he always tried to find the shared ground between Scripture, on the one hand, and culture, idealism, and cynicism on the other.

All his life, Niebuhr was a powerful voice for social justice, and his practicality and authenticity have made him an iconic voice in both the social and political conversation in America. In the 2005 *Speaking of Faith* radio program exploring the public theology of Reinhold Niebuhr, journalist Krista Tippett says, "In my experience as an interviewer, Niebuhr is quoted and cited as an influence more often than any other figure on a wide range of topics and by thinkers and activists on the right and the left."[7]

When I read Niebuhr, his balanced, practical, mature, open-eyed, honest theology leaps off the page. He spent a great deal of time and energy thinking about what it means to hold spiritual ideals in one hand and human realities in the other. Niebuhr described this as a "tension," saying, "Human beings live in the tension between nature and spirit, between knowledge of our mortality and our intimations of transcendent meaning. Our highest hope and calling is to live responsibly in this tension."[8]

When I reflect on Niebuhr and analyze culture, I wonder what it would look like if we were to be practical, mature, open-eyed, and honest about our theology, given the landscape of our culture? What would we see? What would that mean for our spirituality?

Do we flatten contemporary culture in our minds the same way we flatten the Roman Empire?

OUR CULTURAL LANDSCAPE: THREE CHARACTERISTICS

Three defining features of our current cultural landscape include: (1) fast-moving conversations, (2) unlimited possibility, and (3) Peep Culture. Let's look at each.

FAST-MOVING CONVERSATIONS

Our conversations move *very* quickly these days. We live in a world of sound bites, where even serious news on important issues is reduced to stories lasting mere minutes. A long-lasting social media trend is anything over five days.

Recent studies showed that the average attention span at present is just five minutes long; ten years ago, it was twelve minutes.[9] Social media exemplifies this trend: Facebook now owns over 25 percent of total time spent on mobile applications,[10] and the average Facebook user spends more than fifteen hours and thirty-three minutes each month writing and interacting in sound bites.[11]

I love the positive advantages of social media: the ease of spreading thoughts and ideas; the ease of connectivity with friends, family, and people from around the world; and the speed and immediacy of having news and information. In fact, it's even been influential in the overthrow of totalitarian regimes in the Middle East.

In certain realms speed is appropriate. G. K. Chesterton wrote in his essay "Alarms and Discursions" (1910), "Poets have been mysteriously silent on the subject of cheese."[12] I take his argument to mean, beyond the humor of it, that deep things are the territory of the poets. It takes art and space to plumb the depths of a subject. Cursory matters, however, like cheese, can be spoken of easily and quickly; they don't require the depth of poetic diction.

But sometimes there is a real drawback to fast-moving conversations. Whether they concern gun control, the problem of educating our youth, or the nature of sexuality in America, most conversations running their way through the Internet and social media have, far too often, degenerated into a mire of pithy (and sometimes not so pithy) rhetoric and hollow opinion.

Meaningful conversation has devolved to millions of people throwing around pictures, sound bites, and narrow conclusions on topics about which they have not afforded themselves the time for study or reflection.

The death of slow conversation and reflection means the death of interaction and deep exploration. What we are left with when everyone is trading conclusions is simply a choice between two sides of a conversation or argument.[13]

- This issue or that issue
- Conservative or liberal
- Right or wrong
- With me or against me

What we need these days is not an increase in provocative conclusions, but a growth in compelling explanations.

There is a fine texture to deep and original thinking. Deep reflection and sustained dialogue lead to conclusions that are owned and understood. But the death of deep conversation leaves us all victim to the tyranny of triviality.

We are forced by the nature of fast-moving conversations to accept or reject, without the time for the argument and analysis necessary to sufficiently and appropriately support our conclusions.

In his book *The Irony of American History*, Niebuhr said, "Nothing that is worth doing can be achieved in our lifetime."[14] I think he's touching on both the futility of fast-moving conversation *and* the fact that we think we can accomplish big things quickly . . . what I like to refer to as the lie of Unlimited Possibility.

Deep conversation that leads to deep change *takes time*.

UNLIMITED POSSIBILITY

If you really wanted to badly enough, you could be eating dinner in the shadow of the Eiffel Tower in Paris by midnight. Or standing at the top of the Empire State Building.

With our advanced technology today, the sky is the limit, or so it seems. We are consumed with pursuing our passions, chasing our dreams, and seizing opportunities to fulfill our wants and desires. This is fueled by many things, including the mobility of society, the ability to transplant and change jobs, urbanization, and the growth of multiculturalism.

When I was a youth pastor, I frequently showed my students excerpts from movies like *The Count of Monte Cristo* or *The Mask of Zorro*. Both films portray classic scenes in which the would-be hero (think Antonio Banderas) is mentored by a patient, elder instructor in the art of swordsmanship. The scenes usually last around five minutes, during which the bumbling young protagonist—barely able to hold a sword or assume the correct fighting stance—is miraculously transformed into the world's greatest swordsman.

After the clip, I would ask students what they had learned. The obvious takeaways were offered up: "You need a teacher to help you learn," "Practice makes perfect," and so on. When they ran out of answers I would ask them again, and they'd look at me, puzzled, wondering what I had in mind.

"You learned that you can become a world-class expert in five minutes," I would say.

The media age has shaped our perspective, convincing us that there are no limits on what we can do or how much we can accomplish. We believe we can be anyone and do anything—all in a matter of weeks or even minutes.

At the same time globalization has brought the world into our living rooms. Have you ever caught yourself wishing you could have several houses all over the world? Distant places, for many Americans, seem as if they are right next door, and globetrotting seems effortless, just a quick search on Kayak or Expedia away.

Can the illusion of unbounded possibility negatively affect the way we see the world? Do the media age and globalization have a dark side?

Consider short-term mission trips. A Princeton University study found that in one year, 1.6 million US church members took mission trips—an average of eight days—at a cost of $2.4 billion.[15] That is a lot of people spending a lot of money to go fix the world. In many ways, we need to applaud the fact that so much energy is going toward changing the world. But we also need to take a critical look to make sure we're creating deep, lasting relationships and change rather than building a form of justice-tourism.

One good thing about the media age is that it provides us with a virtual window into the atrocities occurring in many places around the globe. But because of what I call the "Midnight in Paris" mentality—that we could be dining on the Avenue des Champs-Élysées tonight if we left right now—that comes along with it, we often buy into the illusion that we can simply hop in and resolve the mess. We see it, we think we know everything about it, and we have been trained to believe we can fix it overnight.

But we are mistaken. Not only can we not fix every issue in a day; we can also become too distracted by what we think we know. When we get caught up in our obsession with other places, other issues, and other contexts, we sometimes forget to pay attention to our own place, issues, and context.

Nicholas Wolterstorff tells the story of Miss Ansel, a woman who owned a large Victorian house in Britain with a large apple orchard in the backyard.[16] Long ago, Wolterstorff and his wife rented the second story of the house along with a young, very poor Jewish couple.

The year was 1956, and Russia had just invaded Hungary. Incensed, Miss Ansel spent an entire day sitting at her desk, writing letters to various world leaders, including the US president and the British prime minister. She told the prime minister that she was even willing to lay her body across the tracks to prevent the Russian trains from entering Hungary if the government would send her there.

Later that year, the apples began to fall in her apple orchard. The poor Jewish couple asked Miss Ansel if they could pick some of the apples. Her answer? "NO! The garden is off-limits to renters." Miss Ansel had a taste for grandiose, exotic justice, but not for the small, pedestrian justice of simple kindness, selflessness, and compassion.

Following God does not have to be exotic to be important. We can't ignore urgent issues at home, like homelessness or the plight of undocumented immigrants, in favor of overseas causes that might seem more exciting or heroic to our American eyes and ears.

PEEP CULTURE: THE NEW VOYEURISM

The history behind the phrase *Peeping Tom* is an interesting one. It comes from a legendary story during the life of Lady Godiva in the eleventh century. As the story goes, Lady Godiva's husband promised to lower taxes if she would ride through town on a horse, naked, wearing nothing but her long hair. Lady Godiva sent word through the town for everyone to be indoors at a certain time so she could ride through the town with privacy. However, a butcher named Tom drilled a hole in his shutter so he could watch her ride by. That's how the phrase *Peeping Tom* became associated with voyeurism.

Until recently, voyeurism, or being a Peeping Tom, was universally looked down on within our culture. The advent of social media and reality TV, however, has created what author Hal Niedzviecki calls the new *Peep Culture*—a culture where the whole paradigm has flipped and we can almost universally peek into the private lives of others. Phrases like, "You're such a stalker" and "You were totally creeping on her" have become commonplace buzz phrases regarding our online social habits. And strangely, today, we find the notion more laughable than repulsive. In a culture that has wholeheartedly embraced the social media frenzy, being a "creep" isn't that unusual. In fact, it's fairly acceptable behavior. It's all made possible because we and everyone else have bought into the trend to broadcast the details of our lives to the world, to spill our guts about anything and everything. No filter. No regrets.

But maybe there is more harm involved in shameless self-exposure than we would like to acknowledge.

Niedzviecki wrote that the Era of Peep Culture—a "rapidly emerging phenomenon, a cultural movement steeped in and made possible by technological change"—has wrought an intrinsic shift in the way we function as a global society at every level and sphere of interaction. "How we socialize, shop, play, date, mate and maybe even process information are all undergoing fundamental transformation."[17]

It would have been an oddity to predict, even twenty-five years ago, that a single person could virtually thumb through hundreds of potential partners, their suggested compatibility based on things like preferred hair color and a favorite hockey team.

Peep Culture has been built on the foundation of fast-moving conversation and unlimited possibility. According to Niedzviecki, there has been a dramatic trend toward narcissism in those who have grown up amid the inundation of social media. One study shows that half a century ago, a grandiose 12 percent of teenagers thought of themselves as "pretty important." Today, however, more than double that number of teens (31 percent) actually believe they one day will be famous, and more than double *that* number (80 percent) consider themselves "truly important."[18]

Peep Culture also has influenced the perpetual growth of moral ambiguity within our culture. It is easy to take for granted the details of lives that are always available to us and everyone else, details that provide a closeness we did not have to earn. One tragic example is the story of a nineteen-year-old who took his own life on a live web stream while chat room participants watched it happen without any urgent sense to intervene. As Niedzviecki put it, that's "what happens when the banality of existence is merged with the inherent excitement of voyeurism."[19]

How do we pay attention to the kingdom of God inside us in the midst of the ever-growing distraction outside of us? How do we value men and women made in the image of God and love our neighbor when he or she is reduced to online chatter and subject matter?

LIFE WITHOUT PRINCIPLE

The media age and globalization are here to stay, so how do we learn to ground ourselves in reality without killing our imaginations or hiding in a cave? Short of becoming a mystic and living out in the desert *sans* Facebook, *sans* Internet, *sans* cell phone, how can we live well without being overwhelmed by speed, unlimited possibility, and peep?

When I was in my twenties, I spent two years of my life journaling. It was a season of life-change and course correction.

What I learned while practicing the disciplines of solitude and writing was the amount of noise that exists. A lot passes for news in life, but a worthy headline is one that is still around after thirty days. I stopped read-ing newspapers and endeavored to attune my ears only to conversations I knew would endure or were significant enough to compel my attention.

During that time, I read Henry David Thoreau's *Walden* for the first time. At the end of my copy of the book was a short essay by Thoreau, titled "Life Without Principle." I returned to that essay many times.

Thoreau began by writing, "Let us consider the way in which we spend our lives. This world is a place of business. What an infinite bustle! . . . It interrupts my dreams. There is no Sabbath."[20]

Later, he tackled the topic of news and information by stating, "We rarely meet a man who can tell us any news which he has not read in a newspaper, or been told by his neighbor . . . You may depend on it, that the poor fellow who walks away with the greatest number of letters, proud of his extensive correspondence, has not heard from himself this long while.[21]

If Thoreau were alive today, he might have written that the poor fellow who spends the most time online has not heard from him- or herself in a long time. Conclusions aplenty; deep thought, maybe less so.

If we do not understand the cultural landscape and cannot critique it, we will continue to suffer from an undiagnosed ailment. The world will lead us into frustration, anxiety, and depression because we cannot win the cultural game. If we are sucked into anything but God's kingdom, we will be chasing after the wind. This is the ailment of our culture.

Niebuhr's words are relevant to those seeking balance in a fast-talking, endlessly possible, voyeuristic world: "The final wisdom of life requires not the annulment of incongruity but the achievement of serenity within and above it."[22]

Niebuhr's words resonate loudly in today's justice-minded culture. They speak to personal responsibility and the need to take action within the subtleties of our day-to-day life and relationships.

Balance is found in grounding our contentment in reality and gaining the ability to bridge the paradox of the infinite with the finite, in the ability to live in the tension between actual and potential—between realism and idealism. An excited realism keeps us from being tyrannized by the possible.

Contentment requires we grasp hold of the actual state of our life, and justice demands we slow down and go deeper. With all that's possible, may we wisely use media and the positive side of globalization to love others and create lasting change in a flat and interconnected world.

CULTURAL DRAMAMINE

Maybe you've felt a little lost or overwhelmed in this age of speed, unlimited possibility, and peep. Or, you have been overcome by the depression, futility, and pressure that come from being inundated by so much information and clamor. Perhaps you've been feeling for a while that something was wrong in church, or with Christian music, or within your Christian community. Or maybe you have just had a sense that something was wrong but could not put your finger on what it was.

If we're able to diagnose what's happening to us, like Niebuhr, then we will be able to lean into those problems and pressures in faith. But diagnosis can be a scary place to start when we're conditioned to the numbness of media saturation.

My friend Tsh Oxenreider is the nationally recognized author of the blog *The Art of Simple*. She recently posted this story about her son on her Facebook page that she gave me permission to reprint:

> Well, we just had a red-letter appointment. Reed met with an OT, and our suspicions are confirmed: he has Sensory Processing Disorder. This might sound like a bummer, but it's actually really good news! We've suspected something was up for years now, but finally took the encouragement of his speech therapist to get him evaluated. He has a 10-hour evaluation headed his way, but in the meantime, we think we FINALLY have an explanation of his speech delay (among other issues).

I love this line: "This might sound like a bummer, but it's actually really good news!" Diagnosis is a bittersweet form of good news. It can be disappointing, shocking, even devastating; but it's a relief to finally know the truth.

Our culture is what it is, and even when we dress it in Christian clothes, it still lacks meaning and hope. Hopefully even if the diagnosis isn't encouraging, it comes as a relief.

With a diagnosis in hand, we can now look toward a remedy.

In the previous chapter, I mentioned that we needed cultural Dramamine as a medication for our high-speed lives. On long car trips, we let our five-year-old daughter, Ashlin, play on our iPad in the car. Occasionally we have to stop her and tell her to look out the window for a while; if we don't she gets carsick. By watching visual anchor points out the window, she keeps from being upset by all the motion.

I think that is what we need as Christians: some kind of cultural stabilizer or Dramamine to keep our equilibrium in spite of the wild motion we are experiencing. We are trying to move smoothly through our lives, but our cultural landscape keeps pitching us left and right. We need something to level us as we navigate. What are the anchor points that we can build into our worldview that never shift, change, or waver?

After watching movies like *Good Will Hunting* or *Finding Forrester* where unlikely characters seem to effortlessly possess hundreds of years' worth of knowledge, we often walk away trying to figure out how we can become a genius. At the same time, these movies have just taught us we shouldn't have to study or learn anything. We want to have all the gifts without investing anything. We think we can be anybody or do anything, but we often lack the values or virtue to go deep.

If culture creates strange goals for us, how can we learn to step back and realize we do not need to be Will Hunting? We should be asking, how can we be like Christ?

Instead of scheming to put more travel pins on the world map, how can we be more intentional about where we are and the things God is leading us to?

Instead of looking into other people's lives and making comparisons, maybe we should nurture our own lives. Maybe we would be more like Christ, instead of sitting inert, voyeuristically, not moving forward.

As we deliberately get outside of the trends, foibles, and thinking of modern culture, may we find that we are freed to be more fully human and imagine how to sing a better song. May we grow old enough to read fairy tales once again.

Ultimately, our anchor point has to be trust. Trust that God is good. Trust that God is in control. Trust enough to do what He's asked of us. It's almost as if we cling to trust in the goodness of God as we walk out His calling in our lives, despite the raging cultural change and hostility to faith around us.

Trust is ultimately a borrowed confidence. Too often we want someone to coddle us, to take away our fear or discomfort. We want comfort more than courage.

In the dedication of *The Lion, the Witch and the Wardrobe*, Lewis wrote to his goddaughter Lucy Barfield, after whom one of the main characters was named, "Some day you will be old enough to start reading fairy tales again."[23] As we deliberately get outside of the trends, foibles, and thinking of our own culture, we may find that we are freed to be more fully human, and more fully Christian. Here is a short prayer I once penned while grappling with the needs of the world and my own inadequacy:

Father:

In cities that never sleep, we are tempted to believe we should never stop striving.

In the noise of traffic and the hustle of crowds, our ears are dulled to the cry of the needy and our hearts grow hard to your prompting.

We are tyrannized by possibility.

We are paralyzed by inadequacy.

We are tempted by possessions.

Lord, help us see through Your eyes.

Help our hearts beat for love and justice as does Yours.

God, fill us with knowledge and grant us the wisdom

to avoid distractions
to balance our duties
to continue in faith
Let your love fuel our love.
Give us the strength, supply us with the grace, and arm us with the humility
needed to continue on the path of contentment and the road of justice in this world.

"If you belonged to the world, it would love you as
its own. As it is, you do not belong to the world,
but I have chosen you out of the world."
—John 15:19

MOTHER KIRK

Christian brotherhood is not an ideal which we
must realize; it is rather a reality created by God in
Christ Jesus in which we may participate.[1]
—DIETRICH BONHOEFFER IN *LIFE TOGETHER*

It can be difficult to trust God even though He is trustworthy and dependable. It is infinitely harder to trust people who are not always trustworthy or
dependable. One of the greatest tools for good—and weapons for bad—the
world has ever known is religion. As C. S. Lewis once said, "Of all the bad
men in the world, religious bad men are the worst."[2]

If this is the case, in a world full of broken people, how do we come to
understand the role the local church is supposed to play in the life of someone who is following God? I once heard it said that we see Jesus a lot like we
see Elvis—we love the man, but his fan club scares the hell out of us.

Some of the most common types of people I've encountered in my ministry over the past two decades are people who want to follow Jesus but cannot
handle church or who have been hurt, abused, or repeatedly let down by
those who claim to be Christians. In this context, there is great debate about

the decline in the American church. There is nuance depending on the sector of the church you're looking at or the segment of the population you're talking to. However, one thing not disputed is that overall, religious affiliation is declining while non-association or nonreligious spirituality is increasing. A recent study by Pew Research reveals that religious affiliation in America is very fluid and that America is on the verge of becoming a minority Protestant country. For example, people unaffiliated with a particular faith today is double the number who were not affiliated with a particular faith as a child.[3]

This is paralleled by a rise in goodwill looking for expression outside the church. In fact, at the time I wrote *Pursuing Justice*, 90 percent of the nonprofit organizations in the world had been created in the previous ten years. We have begun to find ways to replace through nonprofits, parachurch organizations, and other community organizations, a lot of the good in the world that the church was supposed to do.

Everyone seems to be asking, "Can't I just have Jesus and not the institutional church?" You could just hang out with Elvis back in the green room and not have to spend time with his crazy fan club, so it seems obvious we could just hang out with Jesus without His followers. Paradoxically, however, the gospel seems to say we can't have Jesus without His people—messy as they are.

WHERE TWO OR THREE ARE GATHERED

People who have attended church for a long while and know scripture often generate arguments for disengaging from regular attendance and church affiliation using Jesus' words in Matthew 18:20, "For where two or three gather in my name, there am I with them."

If we don't need the local church with its buildings, programs, and pastors to have fellowship with Christ, do we really need the church? If church is such a big part of the problem for so many people, isn't there a better solution? Is not the endgame, after all, simply my own personal relationship with God and doing His will?

But Jesus' words in Matthew 18:20 were not referring to the gathering of believers at all. Actually, just by ourselves we carry the Holy Spirit and can commune with God; we don't need to gather together for that to happen. In this passage, Jesus was actually speaking to the process of how to resolve interpersonal conflicts in the body of believers by referencing the Old Testament legal system.

Under Mosaic law, a testimony of two or three witnesses was required in legal or judicial decisions. Jesus was telling His followers that He trusted them to handle disagreements and conflict resolution with maturity. By promising His presence, He was encouraging them by vowing that if they waded into the deep waters of reconciliation and conflict resolution, in His name and for His glory, then He would be with them in that work.

This teaching has absolutely nothing to do with church affiliation or what constitutes the minimum quota for calling a group of friends "church." Nowhere does Peter or Paul say that it's okay to reject the church because of two to three people with whom to meet instead. Being the people of God is not about taking the minimal way out; it is about a community together for God's glory.

WHAT IS THE CHURCH?

God wants you in a local church. The New Testament is resoundingly clear that believers are called to affiliate with a local church assembly. The body of Christ is not merely the *invisible* church (a term introduced during the Reformation to speak of all those who are truly united with God); it is also manifest in the local church or *visible* church. Yes, as Christians we are members of the invisible church, but this is neither a replacement for nor an excuse from participating in a local church.

As Robert Saucy has written in *The Church in God's Program*, "As for membership in an invisible church without fellowship with any local assembly, this concept is never contemplated in the New Testament. The universal church was the universal fellowship of believers who met visibly in local assemblies." He went on to say that "each individual assembly is the church in that place," and that the "local assembly is the one body of Christ particularized in a certain locality."[4]

Neither Jesus nor the apostles imagined a scenario in which believers were not part of a local assembly. The Greek word *ekklesia* is translated as "church" in the New Testament. It appears in the New Testament 114 times and refers to the local assembly 90 times. The word, coming from Old Greek, refers to an assembly that was regarded as existing only when it actually physically assembled. Josephus (who wrote history at the same time that the New Testament was being written) also used the word *ekklesia* 48 times, always referring to an official gathering.

The church is a visible, active community gathering together—an actual, literal assembly that God designed us to participate in. First Corinthians 12:27 could not be more explicit in saying, "Now you are the body of Christ, and each one of you is a part of it."

WHY THE LOCAL CHURCH?

Why do we need the local church and not just a group of our Christian friends? When I was a college pastor for ten years near Biola University, I was asked this question all the time. Biola students were required to attend chapel three times a week, and because they had Christian roommates and a Christian community, they often felt they didn't need to attend a local church in addition to everything else they were doing.

An honest conversation about following Christ—about being a disciple of Christ and walking by faith—when approached biblically necessarily means addressing faith and discipleship in the context of community. It requires understanding what it means to grow in Christ with people in front of us, behind us, serving, supporting, and encouraging us—and with us doing the same in return for them.

To talk about the life of faith in a vacuum—as just between God and me—is equivalent to saying, "Love the Lord your God," and skipping the rest of the commandment, "and love your neighbor as yourself." I love God by loving others, I learn to love God by loving others, and others learn to love others and God through the same activity. The one cannot be divorced from the other.

When we isolate our discipleship from the church, positive resources that God has provided—scriptural teaching, community, worship and prayer, and the meeting of needs through both giving and receiving—are lost.

We also grow through those negative aspects of church that we'd rather not acknowledge. We grow in Christ and grow in love by learning to work with challenging, negative people and stepping into leadership when necessary in order to pour time and wisdom into those less mature in their faith. Tilling the soil is useful toward the harvest, and breaking down a muscle makes it stronger. Much of what can be beautiful through community exists first in the messiness of community.

When we realize the community is imperfect, we also realize that we are part of the imperfection that damages other people. It is easy to hide the junk in my own life that hurts other people when I just make my relationship with God purely about my solitary relationship with Him. In community, my imperfections are reflected back to me.

These negative things—which we sometimes use as excuses for opting out of church—are actually part of the reason we need to be in church. As we learn how to respond to hard people and situations—how to forgive people, how to redeem situations, how to extend grace—we grow more in Christ. When other people extend grace to me and my faults, I see Christ in and through them.

Being part of a messy spiritual family helps me remember that the whole story is much bigger than me. When I live in community, I am forced to make it about the kingdom of God for all people and not the kingdom of God purely for the benefit of me and me alone.

If the conversation is truly about following and becoming like Christ, then we will love His church as He does.

PILGRIM'S REGRESS

In his allegorical novel *The Pilgrim's Regress*, C. S. Lewis used Mother Kirk as a metaphor to describe the role of the church in the life of the believer (*kirk* is the Scottish word for *church*).

When the main character, John, first learns of Mother Kirk, it is through rumors about her, most of which center on the fact that she is a little bit crazy. When he actually encounters Mother Kirk on his journey, she offers to help him along the way, but he rejects her help. He refuses to be put under anyone else's authority and believes, because he has made it thus far, he can certainly do it all on his own. Plus, she is obviously insane.

Sound familiar?

But eventually, after John has tried everything to complete the journey on his own, he humbly returns to Mother Kirk.

> "I have come to give myself up," he said.
>
> "It is well," said Mother Kirk. "You have come a long way round to reach this place, whither I would have carried you in a few moments."[5]

John had tried everything of the world within his own power and reason to reach the end of his journey, but Mother Kirk could have led him there so much sooner had he just given up his own will. That is what the church teaches us and calls us to do. The church does not save us, but it does play an important role in guiding and connecting us to the One who does save us—the church leads us to Christ and keeps our focus on Him.

TERMINAL CHRISTIANS

There are people who call themselves Christians who are on an inevitable path to walking away from the church and God.

I call these people *terminal Christians*.

In the past, when America was a much more culturally Christian nation, there was really no reason to give up church or Christianity. This was true even if a person wasn't really a believer (we'd say he "isn't walking with the Lord right now"). A person who had no faith would simply live one way on Sundays and holidays and a different way during the week. Hypocrisy was a coping mechanism.

In today's culture—certainly in the Northwest, where I live—if someone doesn't really believe in God and have a mature relationship with Him, there is no reason to attend church. Church has come to be seen as a hierarchical and patriarchal institution that uses people, abuses people, and applies guilt as a means of controlling people's moral lives.

Thus, when I see someone in the church who is beginning to develop a critical view of church (essentially, to adopt culture's view of church), I know I am looking at a "terminal Christian." That individual might not be dead yet, but she is on a trajectory that leads to separation from the people of God, and separation from the people God has identified with will ultimately mean separation from God Himself.

And separation from God is death.

Don't get me wrong: if someone has a real faith, then I believe that faith will continue to grow and develop. What I'm talking about are people who have simply been a part of the herd, but who will soon find their way out. The frustrating part is that terminal Christianity also exposes just how many people in our churches have never really "gotten it." They have followed pastors or teachers and have been entertained by programs and music, but they have never truly become disciples of Christ (what is meant by the word *Christian*).

Jesus said, "Seek and you will find" (Matthew 7:7). He meant to convey that our honest pursuit of God will be rewarded.

I realize, by watching terminal Christians, that the opposite is also true. If someone is looking to find his way out of church and away from God, that person will find plenty of excuses to leave. We will find what we seek.

An article in *Christianity Today* entitled "When Are We Going to Grow Up? The Juvenilization of American Christianity," details some of the historical trends in culture and the church that have led to immaturity in faith. According to this article it began in the 1940s and 1950s, when churches and other groups developed youth programs to capture the passion of youth so future generations could guard and redeem American Christianity.[6]

A large portion of evangelicalism was largely successful in this effort, and certainly positive things have come from it. However, the negative side effect has been a generation of Christians who have grown up still possessing an adolescent faith. They see their faith as a means to make them feel better, cope with stress, and bring personal fulfillment.

While these elements are certainly benefits of a relationship with Christ, we cannot neglect the fact that it is we who follow Christ, not the other way around. Discipleship means submitting ourselves to Christ for the long haul, not for a quick fix or emotional high. We do not just go to church for therapy. A relationship with Christ is bigger than our felt needs.

CONSUMER CHRISTIANITY

As a culture of consumption takes root in churches and Christianity, our view of church and the value placed on our commitment to the local body is effectively distorted.

In *The Screwtape Letters* C. S. Lewis uses Screwtape (a fictional devil who tries to teach his devil nephew how to ensure a man's eternal damnation), to highlight truths by showing how culture often matches what the devil would advise. In one section where Screwtape is coaching his nephew on how to prevent a human from going to church he writes, "Surely you know that if a man can't be cured of churchgoing, the next best thing is to send him all over the neighborhood looking for the church that 'suits' him until he becomes a taster or connoisseur of churches . . . [for] the search for a 'suitable' church makes the man a critic."[7]

Unfortunately, doesn't this describe perfectly much of modern church-going?

When we become connoisseurs of church, it is no longer about the stewardship of our gifts and influence. It is no longer about building each other up and growing together into maturity and knowledge of Christ. We become self-focused and make church exclusively about our experience. We criticize people, services, worship styles, and sermons rather than loving others and looking for ways to grow and equip one another as Christians. Or, as Eugene Cho has put it, we become guests rather than hosts.[1]

In Ephesians 4:11–13, Paul shared Christ's goal for the church: "So

Christ himself gave the apostles, the prophets, the evangelists, the pastors and teachers, to equip his people for works of service, so that the body of Christ may be built up until we all reach unity in the faith and in the knowledge of the Son of God and become mature."

He continued with his dreams for the church, "speaking the truth in love, we will grow to become in every respect the mature body of him who is the head, that is, Christ. From him the whole body, joined and held together by every supporting ligament, grows and builds itself up in love, as each part does its work" (vv. 15–16).

Quite the opposite of a consumer Christianity, Christians are to help each other reach unity, become mature, and grow into the fullness of Christ.

In a unique and profound way, God uses the local church to speak to us and shape us; likewise, He uses each one of us and our individual gifts and wisdom to shape the church as part of our service to others. My participation with a church cannot be divorced from my influence on others and their influence on me.

The church is not just a mechanical or spiritual device. It is a family with all the fullness, mystery, and beauty that can only exist in a sacred community. God's idea and our opportunity is to go beyond taking the church purely as an individual or consumer. The church is meant to be a group of individuals, diverse across all spectrums, including gender, race, socioeconomic status, and age, coming together as a family.

When we treat the local gathering of believers lightly and elevate other organizations above it, we devalue the spiritual family God envisioned and created in His great love for us. We must put down deep roots and have a deep enough conversation to work through the issues of the church rather than avoiding the church and its complexities.

BURNED OUT ON RELIGION?

Eugene Peterson is a Greek and Hebrew scholar well known for his paraphrase of the Bible called *The Message*. He began translating the Psalms because he saw that the English translation often sanitized the energy, desperation, and cries in them. After translating the Psalms, he moved on to the rest of the Bible.

I love his translation of Matthew 11:28–30. The passage became a major building block of our goals as we started Antioch: "Are you tired? Worn out? Burned out on religion? Come to me. Get away with me and you'll recover your life. I'll show you how to take a real rest. Walk with me and work with me—watch how I do it. Learn the unforced rhythms of grace. I won't lay anything heavy or ill-fitting on you. Keep company with me and you'll learn to live freely and lightly."

This passage continues to shape me. The phrase "burned out on religion" has grown in importance for me over time.

When I was studying engineering, I did an internship at a company that manufactures flow meters. One semester I helped them update their quality assurance documents in order to stay compliant with various guidelines and maintain a quality business rating. As part of this work, I spent weeks writing hundreds of detailed policies for different departments.

The head of our department would walk around and shake hands with everyone once a day. One day he stopped me and said, "I got to see your presentation on the things you're working on. It is well written, creative, and detailed. But it's not good at all."

He pointed out that I was missing the big picture. Making too many guidelines that weren't necessary would make business that much harder for everyone. The goal wasn't to create more to-dos and check boxes, but to pare it down to the essential things required to meet quality and compliance standards.

It is the same thing we do with church and Christianity. Churches often come together and try to keep everyone compliant with their dominant values. Churches like this end up wounding the people they are supposed to help.

But Jesus says, "Come to me, all you who are weary" (Matthew 11:28). He came to bring grace instead of judgment, but often when people come to church, they don't find grace and rest.

As the body of Christ, we assist in bringing people to the head, who is Christ. Sometimes we help in that process, sometimes we get in the way of that process, and sometimes we do damage in the process.

Life is messy. We don't always get it right, yet in all of the messiness, God is faithful. God uses us to love each other and minister to each other. In spite of the challenges of church and faith, we can introduce people to the One who is the source of life and salvation for all of us.

One of the most difficult paradoxes of faith is that in some strange way, we need to be around unhealthy people to get healthy. We need to be around messy people to begin the process of becoming clean.

CHOOSING CHURCH

Maybe you have suffered in the church; maybe you have given up. Your pain is real, and I understand that and grieve with you. But the church needs you, and you need it—both in the universal and local sense.

No church is perfect because it is made up of imperfect, sinful people. Antioch Church is not perfect, and I am sure we have unintentionally hurt people along the way, but we exist believing that we can redeem the local church and create a healthy community. We believe it's better to find our-selves in a family, even if it is a bit dysfunctional, than to find ourselves alone in the world. We believe that our opportunity to serve and influence others is every bit as much of a consideration as our own experience or felt needs with regard to church.

People ask me why I continue to champion the local church. At the end of the day, I don't think we can fully experience the Christian life and the greatest of God's blessing if we neglect the local church.

I love the local church not because I am a pastor; rather, I am a pastor because I love the local church.

Together, may we find a renewed passion for how we can lead and redeem the local church in America.

On arriving there, they gathered the church together
and reported all that God had done.
—Acts 14:27

OUTSIDE LOOKING IN

In sorrow we must go, but not in despair. Behold!
We are not bound for ever to the circles of the world,
and beyond them is more than memory.[1]
—J. R. R. TOLKIEN

If you visit the museum at ancient Corinth, or Delphi, or the Acropolis Museum in Athens, you're likely to find on display a hand mirror from the time of Christ and the early church. Several have survived from that period, though it is likely they were owned only by the affluent. Such mirrors were made from an imperfectly flattened hunk of bronze. In shape, they were similar to a modern hand mirror, but what would have been reflected back from them would have been not much more than a blurred and indistinct outline.

These mirrors are very different from the modern mirror with which we are all familiar, and in which the reflection we see is—while not the real thing—a near-perfect likeness. Modern optics (and vanity lighting) make for extremely accurate reflections.

It is this ancient bronze hand mirror to which Paul alluded in his letter to the Corinthian church to illustrate the difference between our present experience and our future realization of the realities of God, His love for us, and the good He has in store for us: "Now we see but a poor reflection as in a mirror; then we shall see face to face. Now I know in part; then I shall know fully, even as I am fully known" (1 Corinthians 13:12).

If we picture a modern mirror, it robs Paul's illustration of its force. His point was that the reality of eternity with God—of heaven—is far, far beyond our present ability to comprehend. We can only see (as the King James Version has it) "through a glass, darkly."

THROUGH A GLASS, DARKLY

Heaven is a foggy concept that is often mischaracterized or oversimplified. We tend not to think deeply about it even though it is a weighty, ultimate matter.

At the end of his life, the apostle Paul was lying in a prison cell, waiting to be executed. As he pondered his life and wrote good-byes to his loved ones, he penned these famous words to his friend Timothy: "For I am already being poured out like a drink offering, and the time for my departure is near. I have fought the good fight, I have finished the race, I have kept the faith. Now there is in store for me the crown of righteousness, which the Lord, the righteous Judge, will award to me on that day—and not only to me, but also to all who have longed for his appearing" (2 Timothy 4:6–8).

Paul was very concerned about heaven and the connection between his walk of faith here and eternity.

But isn't everyone thinking about heaven when they're about to die? Why should we think or talk about heaven now? Especially in a book about faith?

We may not be able to perfectly understand the ideas of heaven, the afterlife, and the immortality of human souls, but we do need to consider them for several reasons:

- Heaven and eternal life are central themes of Christianity.
- The existence of the afterlife is the only thing that provides a

resolution for the concept of human responsibility regarding justice and injustice.

• Jesus and the apostles used heaven as a primary motivation. Throughout the church age, Christian thinkers and teachers have followed their example in this regard.

• While there may be much we can't comprehend about these things, there's also much mistaken belief about them (in our secular culture and in our churches) that we can dispel with a good deal of confidence.

We cannot—as finite people—fully understand the infinite. As creatures confined by space and time, we can't really grasp realities that involve different dimensions.

C. S. Lewis put it this way: "The human soul was made to enjoy some object that is never fully given—nay, cannot even be imagined as given—in our present mode of subjective and spatio-temporal experience."[2]

We'll see later that heaven might be a much more physical, earthly place than we imagined. But to understand the connection between heaven and our walk of faith, we need to understand the eternal, spiritual part of us: our soul.

UNDERSTANDING WHO WE ARE

People are becoming increasingly familiar with stories of near-death experiences, especially with the recent book *Heaven Is for Real*, which tells the story of a young boy, Colton Burpo, and his trip to heaven and back during an emergency surgery.

Many people read such stories with skepticism and often find them hard to believe. That's partly because in our culture it is popular to believe that we are purely physical beings, nothing more than brains and bodies. That even our mental lives—our thoughts, beliefs, memories, desires, and such—are somehow reducible to the firing of neurons in our brains. This view—generally referred to as *physicalism*—is in stark opposition with the biblical view of humanity.

The existence of near-death experiences,[3] common sense and human experience, philosophical scrutiny, and recent developments in neuroscience all seem to indicate that we are more than a product of electrochemical reactions.[4] Summarizing his research, Wilder Penfield, the father of neurosurgery, wrote, "To expect the highest brain mechanism or any set of reflexes, however complicated, to carry out what the mind does, and thus perform all the functions of the mind, is quite absurd."[5]

When it comes to understanding who we are, there is more than can be measured with a microscope. We commonly refer to this "something more" as our soul, the eternal part of us that cannot be seen, measured, or killed.

But even those of us who believe in the soul can be influenced by the *physicalism* in our culture. We have a tendency to overemphasize our material aspects to the relative disregard of our immaterial—the soulish and spiritual—aspects of personhood.

This can be seen in our culture's fixation on youth, athletics, and beauty. We appropriately celebrate birth and babies, but we hide from death, disease, and old age. All of the "big events" on which we focus—sports championships, graduation, prom, marriage, kids—are associated with being young, and we do our best to remain in that life stage.

Instead of viewing our physical being as dominant and our spiritual life as ethereal, we need to find a more balanced biblical view that holds in tension our physical reality *and* our spiritual reality.

A more biblical (and human) understanding would embrace the entire arc of life. It would see age as of great worth, possessing inner beauty and wisdom as supreme assets, and—like Paul in his letter to Timothy—would see this life as an upward trajectory, always with the goal of experiencing the eternal reality of heaven and intimacy with God.

Thus, heaven confronts us with another paradox in the life of faith: that we are *both* physical and spiritual. We can't emphasize one of our dimensions at the expense of the other.

George MacDonald, the famous Scottish pastor and author (1824–1905), addressed this. In his fictional *Annals of a Quiet Neighborhood*, he has the elderly and failing Mrs. Tomkins lamenting, "But, you know, sir, everybody dies. I *must* die, and be laid in the churchyard, sir. And that's what I don't like." To this, the young vicar (the writer of the annals) replies, "But I say that is all a mistake. *You* won't die. Your body will die, and be laid away out of sight; but you will be awake, alive, more alive than you are now, a great deal." The vicar then adds parenthetically:

> And here let me interrupt the conversation to remark upon the great mistake of teaching children that they have souls. The consequence is, that they think of their souls as of something which is not themselves. For what a man *has* cannot be himself. Hence, when they are told that their souls go to heaven, they think of their *selves* as lying in the grave. They ought to be taught that they have bodies; and that their bodies die; while they themselves live on. Then they will not think, as old Mrs. Tomkins did, that *they* will be laid in the grave. It is making altogether too much of the body, and is indicative of an evil tendency to materialism, that we talk as if we *possessed* souls, instead of *being* souls. We should teach our children to think no more of their bodies when dead than they do of their hair when it is cut off, or of their old clothes when they have done with them.[6]

Far from being merely bodies and brains, we are souls who presently have bodies. We are souls who will continue our temporal walk of faith into eternity. Our souls survive the death of our bodies, and someday we will each be given a new, resurrected body.

Even Jesus seemed to point out that reality is more than this physical universe. In Luke 23:43, Jesus comforted the thief on the cross next to Him with the promise of something greater: "Truly I tell you, today you will be with me in paradise."

Dwight L. Moody, the famous twentieth-century Christian evangelist, said it well. He stated, "Someday you will read in the papers that Moody is dead. Don't you believe a word of it. At that moment I shall be more alive than I am now. I was born of the flesh in 1837; I was born of the spirit in 1855. That which is born of the flesh may die. That which is born of the Spirit shall live forever."[7]

TEN THOUSAND YEARS ON STREETS OF GOLD?

When cultural stereotypes catch on, they have the power to obscure truth.

For years, my picture of heaven was a bunch of people sitting around on a cloud, playing harps. And I wasn't too excited about it. My picture was based on hundreds of stereotypical paintings, cartoons, and commercials about heaven I'd seen throughout my life.

But what if art has failed us? What if it has been a bad teacher when it comes to the subject of heaven? What if heaven defies artistic representation?

And what if we have misunderstood the scriptural references to heaven?

God often puts marvelous realities into word pictures far beyond our imaginations that enable us to catch a glimmer of the truth. If we take these word pictures concretely ("literally," in modern usage), we will be in error, and we're likely to miss the greater glories to which they point.

One of these word pictures is a passage from Revelation 21:21, a reference to the New Jerusalem: "The great street of the city was of pure gold." I think the imagery here is creative hyperbole. I don't think God wants us to expect literal streets of the element known to chemists as Au. Rather, He is trying to enable us to grasp visions of glory unimaginable.

The streets of New Testament times were simply dust or perhaps rock in some places in the Roman world—the most abundant and worthless of materials. In the greater world awaiting us, everything will be so glorious that it will be as though gold (the most precious commodity in our present experience) is relatively worthless in that royal economy.

Another example of a creative word picture is the Messianic prophecy of Isaiah 11:6–7: "The wolf will live with the lamb, the leopard will lie down with the goat, the calf and the lion and the yearling together; and a little child will lead them. The cow will feed with the bear, their young will lie down together, and the lion will eat straw like the ox."

This Hebrew poetry is declaring that the future reign of the Messiah (the "Branch of Jesse") will be characterized by a level of peace and harmony that is currently inconceivable to us. The wolf-and-lamb word picture is the

Holy Spirit's way of putting the reality of infinite peace in practical terms that are understandable to finite minds.

We also experience a good deal of confusion with regard to time and eternity. In this creation, we experience time in a very specific way, and we find it difficult (if not impossible) to imagine things otherwise. We naturally think of eternity in heaven as being composed of days or years like those we experience now, only with the difference that those days go on and on forever. For example, the lyrics "When we've been there ten thousand years . . ." come from "Amazing Grace," a song that's became one of the most treasured hymns of Christendom.

But time itself is merely a dimension of the created universe of which we are a part. We measure days and years by the behavior of our solar system. A day is a complete revolution of the earth on its axis, and a year is the time taken by the earth to orbit the sun.

The motion of the earth may not apply to eternity.

While here, we won't ever know how time is going to work in eternity. Our current predicament of being confined to the time of this universe will continue to make it hard for us to imagine existing outside of it.

But you don't need to be worried about sitting on a cloud, bored out of your mind for all eternity, caught in a loop day after day after day of playing a harp or singing. What Isaiah and John were getting at is that heaven will be completely different from life here—a surprise, not a disappointment.

GOOGLE MAPS WON'T GET YOU TO HEAVEN

As physical beings located in space, we very naturally default to thinking of heaven as a place or location. We are encouraged in this vision, since Scripture's portrayals necessarily involve spatial imagery that comports with our experience of *this* world.

What if heaven is not so much a different place as a different way of existing?

Take one of Jesus' illustrations (recorded in John 14:2): "In my Father's house are many rooms; if it were not so, I would have told you. I am going there to prepare a place for you." In America, many of us live in one or more houses with only our immediate family (or maybe some roommates). Our parents and grandparents have their own houses, and we expect our children to have their own space someday. We may have rooms for cooking, for dining, for sleeping, for watching television . . .

When we read Jesus' words, we tend to think He is promising us a fifteen-by-twelve-foot room in which we get to hang our own pictures and stay up as late as we want reading a book.

But for Jesus' Jewish listeners, the house was a multigenerational dwelling where extended family were commonly in residence and honored guests were accommodated and made to feel like family.

In its proper context, Jesus' illustration was simply a way of reaffirming the Father's intention of reconciling to Himself as sons and daughters all those who enter into relationship with His eternal Son.

Rather than promising us a room in a big house, Jesus is saying that we'll be part of the family. Toward the end of His prayer for His followers, Jesus said, "May they be brought to complete unity to let the world know that you sent me and have loved them even as you have loved me. Father, I want those you have given me to be with me where I am, and to see my glory, the glory you have given me because you loved me before the creation of the world" (John 17:23–24).

Near the beginning of this same prayer, He said, "Now this is eternal life: that they may know you, the only true God, and Jesus Christ, whom you have sent" (v. 3).

Heaven is a *relational* reality, not just a place in the sky. Eternal life is a relational reality, not a period of time. How would that change the way we live our lives if we lived as though eternity started now? How would we change our current relationships if we viewed them as eternal? How would it affect the decisions we make?

Paul saw "keeping the faith" as directly tied to heaven, a continuation of the relationship he had spent his whole life cultivating. He understood the connection between what we do with our bodies and decision making during this life and our eternal relationship with our Father.

ETERNITY STARTS NOW

If heaven is more accurately understood as a relational reality, in the same way hell should be recognized not as a place but as a cessation of relationship. Existence in hell entails being cut off from friends and loved ones and, more importantly, it means being cut off from the love of the One who created us to find our joy in intimate relationship with Him. As George MacDonald put it, "The one principle in hell is—'I am on my own.'"[8]

The banishment of Adam and Eve from the garden of Eden and the loss of intimacy with God they had enjoyed there is a picture of the eternal banishment from God's presence that awaits those humans who choose to reject His offer of love and forgiveness.

Where heaven entails a restoration of relationship with our Creator, hell is existence apart from God.

As with the word pictures for heaven, the Bible's word pictures describing hell (darkness, fire, gnashing of teeth) probably are not meant to be taken literally. Nonetheless, the reality of hell is worse than we can presently imagine, just as the reality of heaven is far better than our finite minds can comprehend.

Mark Twain had a funny take on our confusion about the afterlife: "Go to heaven for the climate, hell for the company."[9] But if we accurately understand heaven as fundamentally relational, and hell as absence of relationship, then we can also recognize that *eternity starts now*. For those of us who will spend eternity with God, eternal life doesn't begin at death; instead, it begins when we enter into relationship with the Son of God, at salvation, when we are adopted into the family of God.

According to C. S. Lewis, "Heaven enters wherever Christ enters, even in this life."[10] He fleshed out his thinking, saying, "Earth, I think, will not be found by anyone to be in the end a very distinct place. I think earth, if chosen instead of Heaven, will turn out to have been, all along, only a region in hell: and earth, if put second to Heaven, to have been from the beginning a part of Heaven itself."[11]

THE NEW CREATION

A truly biblical understanding acknowledges both our material and immaterial components, but sees them holistically. Just as we can fall into the cultural temptation to overemphasize physical reality, we can sometimes fall into the religious trap of overemphasizing spiritual reality.

God designed us to inhabit both.

In the creation account of Genesis 1, God was most pleased with the creation in its entirety: "God saw all that he had made, and it was very good" (v. 31).

In Paul's letter to the Colossians, we read that "all things, whether things on earth or things in heaven" are being reconciled to the Father through Jesus (1:20). While we may be tempted to spiritualize this passage, to claim that "all things" really just means human souls, the passage does not allow this. The "all things" that Christ came to redeem are the same "all things" that—earlier in the same paragraph—Christ created (v. 16), and preceded and sustains (v. 17).

Heaven and hell provide an ultimate justice not always realized in this life,[12] but it is equally true that it is in this life that we choose—and are held responsible for our choices—to act justly or not.

At the heart of Christian belief is resurrection, surviving the death of earthly bodies. But it is crucial to note that this is a *bodily* resurrection, and that it does not apply only to immaterial souls.

Read what Paul said in Romans 8:9–11:

You, however, are not in the realm of the flesh but are in the realm of the Spirit, if indeed the Spirit of God lives in you. And if anyone does not have the Spirit of Christ, they do not belong to Christ. But if Christ is in you, then even though your body is subject to death because of sin, the Spirit gives life because of righteousness. And if the Spirit of him who raised Jesus from the dead is living in you, he who raised Christ from the dead will also give life to your mortal bodies because of his Spirit who lives in you.

And later in verse 23:

We ourselves, who have the firstfruits of the Spirit, groan inwardly as we wait eagerly for our adoption to sonship, the redemption of our bodies.

I can't really picture what resurrected bodies will be like, but the early disciples knew *exactly* what to expect. After all, they saw the first one: Jesus.

Jesus' own resurrected body was physical, but not quite the same as the bodies we have now. In John 20:26, the implication is that Jesus passed through walls or a locked door. In Acts 1:9, "he was taken up before their very eyes, and a cloud hid him from their sight."

Luke, who was a physician, recorded several details about Jesus' appearances after His resurrection. There was something about Him that made the disciples think they had seen a ghost, and He did not always obey the physics of this universe. Here's one example:

> While they were still talking about this, Jesus himself stood among them and said to them, "Peace be with you."
>
> They were startled and frightened, thinking they saw a ghost. He said to them, "Why are you troubled, and why do doubts rise in your minds? Look at my hands and my feet. It is I myself! Touch me and see; a ghost does not have flesh and bones, as you see I have." (Luke 24:36–39)

As we saw in the passage from Romans, Paul was convinced that we would be resurrected like Jesus, with renewed, more powerful, more *alive* bodies. That is the hope Paul was trying to point us toward.[13]

N. T. Wright, the renowned Scottish scholar, Anglican minister, and theologian, wrote his entire book *Surprised by Hope* to reframe the way we think about heaven, hell, and the resurrection. I think the following quote is the best summation of the significance of resurrection:

> The point of the resurrection . . . is that the present bodily life is not valueless just because it will die. . . . What you do with your body in the present matters because God has a great future in store for it. . . . What you do in the present—by painting, preaching, singing, sewing, praying,

teaching, building hospitals, digging wells, campaigning for justice, writing poems, caring for the needy, loving your neighbor as yourself—will last into God's future. These activities are not simply ways of making the present life a little less beastly, a little more bearable, until the day when we leave it behind altogether (as the hymn so mistakenly puts it . . .). They are part of what we may call building for God's kingdom.[14]

MacDonald and Moody looked ahead to a paradise outside of this universe. N. T. Wright rests in the promise that heaven and earth will finally be made new through the power of Christ's resurrection.

But both perspectives on eternity require us to take a lot on faith.

NOT WORTH COMPARING

Of course, our earthly experience of the blessedness and joy of eternity in relationship with God is imperfect, and we are distracted by trials and sorrows that won't be part of our future heavenly experience.

A critical part of Christianity's answer to the problem of suffering is the recognition of the biblical truth that our current physical lives are not the final picture. Eternal life and heaven—which are devoid of sorrow and suffering—are the greater realities for which we were created.

Paul reassured the believers in first-century Rome with these words: "I consider that our present sufferings are not worth comparing with the glory that will be revealed in us."[15] To the Corinthians, he put it this way: "For our light and momentary troubles are achieving for us an eternal glory that far outweighs them all."[16] Peter expressed this same idea to the persecuted Christians to which he wrote.[17]

Really? Can we honestly dismiss as "light and momentary" all of the suffering with which we're familiar? Does that include that of the loved one whose entire life has been characterized by the pain of a debilitating disease, the friend whose life was defined by the car crash that took the lives of his wife and children, the village in the Democratic Republic of Congo in which the people have never known a time free from gunfire, murder, rape, and the worst kinds of atrocities?

Paul himself had a pretty close relationship with pain and suffering. A catalog of his experiences (summarized in 2 Corinthians 11:23–29) includes multiple imprisonments, beatings, whippings, and shipwrecks—he faced danger wherever he went. Moreover, the Master for whom he endured all this was—despite living a perfect life and bringing healing and restoration everywhere he traveled—unjustly imprisoned, whipped, spat upon, lied about, and crucified; He was, as foretold about Him in Isaiah 53:3, "a man of sorrows, and familiar with suffering."

The New Testament perspective does not involve a denial of the intense pain and suffering of this life. Rather, it establishes the insignificance of the (presently realized) suffering relative to the (presently unimagined) glory that awaits us. Of course, accepting this as true involves a step of trust.

Faith requires us to hold to the paradox that even in death, there is hope; that in our pain and suffering, there is blessing in store; that though we live in a world held captive by fear and death, in its present state it is not our final home. In faith we step forward while we wait for a new heaven and a new earth.

Getting this right was a primary reason for the spread of Christianity in the first centuries after the resurrection. Along with their great love and compassion, the other defining characteristic of Christians in the Roman world—where they were tortured and killed for their faith—was that they didn't fear death.

This is perhaps best attested by a hostile source, the second-century Greek satirist Lucian, who mockingly described Christians as starting with "the general conviction that they are immortal for all time, which explains the contempt of death and voluntary self-devotion which are so common among them."[18]

Without the resurrection, it's hard to gamble with your life.

The issue of heaven is all about where we draw the finish line. It is about the time and the space that we give for the story to resolve. Heaven is where we look to for our rewards, and for the scales to balance.

HAPPINESS ON THE INSIDE

Heaven is real.

And though eternity starts now, for the moment we stand outside of heaven, trying to get a glimpse of the realities that will be ours for eternity. Our picture of heaven is not the artistic pictures we've seen, but the fullness of relationship we find in being united with God. Heaven provides us with the promise of future rewards and motivates us through the difficult times that, paradoxically, come as we obey God in faith.

Heaven is the promise of being with God, free from pain and sorrow, that serves as the incentive for Christian action and sacrifice.

This life does not afford the reality of complete experienced happiness throughout. Only heaven can afford *secure, eternal, and complete* happiness. This is why happiness is understood as an attitude *and a goal*. Perhaps the simplest way to think of heaven is as a kingdom where happiness and joy are kept on the inside, and strife, envy, evil, suffering, and anti-joy are kept out. A kingdom where we are in perfect harmony with each other and our Creator.

Heaven is permanent happiness that cannot be taken away.

In heaven, happiness is the air that is breathed.

You make known to me the path of life; you will fill me with joy
in your presence, with eternal pleasures at your right hand.
—Psalm 16:11

SPIRITUAL FATIGUE (OR, THE DARK NIGHT OF THE SOUL)

Do not abandon yourselves to despair.
We are the Easter people and hallelujah is our song.[1]
—POPE JOHN PAUL II

In my hometown of Bend, Oregon, it often looks on the surface as though life is easy. Set at the foot of the mountains, with vast blue skies, we have more microbreweries and pubs per capita than anywhere else in America and enough dogs to earn the title "Dogtown USA" from *Dog Fancy* magazine in 2012.[2] It seems like a relaxed place to live. But if you scratch below the surface just a little, you'll find the stress of many here who have never recovered from the economic downturn and the housing market crash. People work hard just to scrape by. Many live in a constant state of stress and panic. Additionally, we have just as high an incidence of disease and divorce as any other town in the States. We have friends with MS, colleagues watching husbands waste away from cancer, and young parents struggling for a diagnosis of their sick children.

Life is tough, and ministering to people who are suffering can be overwhelming.

SUFFERING'S REACH

Even as the promise of heaven grounds us in this world, we still face present trials. Our growth, as Christians, is always preceded by and saturated with risk. No one is exempt from the burden of suffering in this world. Not even those who follow Christ.

Nobody escapes life without going through a valley, a dark place, or a time of deep sorrow. Tragedy and suffering are simply inherent realities of the human experience. Although there has been an upswing of teaching within the global church that sends a contrary message—one that says that the people of God can elude such hardship—it isn't completely true. Certainly God can heal people, bless men and women, and deliver us from hardship, but in the end, at a minimum we will all suffer the death of loved ones and eventually grow old and die ourselves.

I deal regularly with what I would call spiritual fatigue—people who step back from Christianity because life gets to be too difficult or painful. In the intensity of life's turmoil, we are challenged to endure but often burn out and give up.

In Oregon whitewater rafting is a popular activity. When a raft full of people maneuvers a Class 4 rapid, it is expected that some might be bounced overboard by the turbulence, but the further expectation is that all will get back into the raft.

Likewise, in the height of trials, we can become disillusioned, distance ourselves from church and other Christians—even walk away from God entirely. Some of us who get thrown from the raft never make it back.

In *The Screwtape Letters*, C. S. Lewis has the demon Screwtape explaining what might be called the natural undulations of joy and sorrow in the life of humans:

Their nearest approach to constancy, therefore, is undulation—the repeated return to a level from which they repeatedly fall back, a series of troughs and peaks. If you had watched your patient carefully you would have seen this undulation in every department of his life—his interest in his work, his affection for his friends, his physical appetites, all go up and down. As long as he lives on earth periods of emotional and bodily richness and liveliness will alternate with periods of numbness and poverty.[3]

But we do not like ups and downs. We would prefer to be in a state of pleasure or peace all the time.

So we fill our time doing the things that we think make us happy. We read books that tell us life is meant to make us happy. We attend conferences that offer keys to finding happiness. Most importantly, we avoid those things that rob us of the joy and happiness we believe we deserve, whatever it takes.

Now, I'm not saying that joy does not belong to the believer. In fact, the One who calls us to follow Him is joy Himself. Even so, all of us will certainly meet suffering and seasons of drought. These "troughs" of which Lewis wrote are simply part of the natural progression of life.

If we become enchanted by promises of prosperity and endless health, we are setting ourselves up for shocking, unmerciful disappointment. If we anticipate adversity, we will do ourselves a lot of good and grow our ability to persevere in our walk of faith.

Biblical teaching offers the promise of growth as a result of suffering—our affliction is not all in vain. For example, James 1:2–4 says, "Consider it pure joy, my brothers and sisters, whenever you face trials of many kinds, because you know that the testing of your faith produces perseverance. Let perseverance finish its work so that you may be mature and complete, not lacking anything."

How do we find strength by not only expecting, but also truly believing, that our voyage through trials is producing faith in us? How do we know that our seasons of exhaustion and spiritual fatigue are producing something of value?

Bo Stern, a local friend, has written a book on suffering born out of her journey following her husband's diagnosis with ALS. Recently, she remarked, "I used to think that my faith could help me avoid suffering. Lately, I'm learning that there are some things that only suffering can teach or bring about in us. Faith is being willing to walk that road, believing God is working these things together to make us more beautiful, more like His Son."

Not everyone has Bo's maturity and natural positivity. I hope for myself, my family, and the church that we would all be able to have our faith strengthened through trials rather than seeing trials as sufficient reason to walk away from Christian community.

PREPARING FOR SPIRITUAL FATIGUE

My heart's desire as a pastor is that I would help people follow God and find Christian community. I want to equip them to maintain their spiritual resiliency, find healthy fellowship, and create patterns of behavior to sustain their walks of faith through a deep relationship and understanding of God.

Napoleon the Great, French emperor and military leader after the era of the French Revolution, is purported to have said, "The first virtue in a soldier is endurance of fatigue; courage is only the second virtue."[4] When I came across that quote, I realized for the first time the significance of fatigue.

We don't often think of fatigue as a big deal, but if you consider the life of a soldier, the reality of fatigue begins to sink in. When the grinding gears of war turn you, you go through more than just one battle. War is prolonged fighting, sleepless nights compounded one on top of the other, and constant bombardment that wear down your body and spirit.

It is at that crucial moment—the point at which body and soul begin to splinter under the pressure of exhaustion—that true strength is tested.

We will all encounter seasons of spiritual fatigue. Preparing ourselves as Christians is more than simply expecting difficulty. If we are going to bear up in spite of our spiritual weariness, we must tenaciously build up our strength.

Building endurance requires training.

In today's Western culture, however, we tend to understand and care more about our physical stamina than about our spiritual endurance—we spend way more time building physical stamina than building faith that will last. When we do think about spiritual stamina, we are likely to think in terms of safeguarding our successes, blessings, and happiness while avoiding struggles, trials, or dark periods.

If we're going to sustain our Christian walk, how can we prepare for the despair and dryness that will certainly follow close behind those seasons of joy? Our primary concern should not be how to navigate around the desert, but rather where to find water when we're lost in the middle of it.

THE FACES OF FATIGUE

Spiritual fatigue often comes on slowly.

However spiritual fatigue begins, the reality is the same. It depletes you and drains your motivation to continue on. Like climbers succumbing to the elements on Mount Everest, we begin to shut down and give up.

The faces of fatigue are as diverse as the people who wear them and the situations that produce them. For example, those in helping professions, like doctors, aid workers, pastors, and teachers, often experience forms of spiritual fatigue. Help or service workers are constantly pouring out, and only sometimes receiving affirmation.

The paradoxical lesson of faith is that somehow, emptiness can be redeemed. Hardship and toil, if endured, can shape us. Or, as the Old Testament has it, beauty can come from ashes.

To equip ourselves to endure, we need to know how to identify and respond to fatigue. We need to learn to recognize its many faces.

So what exactly does spiritual fatigue look like?

AN ABSENCE OF GOOD

We may have all walked through seasons when it seems as if there is an acute absence of goodness in our lives. These times are daunting as circumstances compound one after another and threaten to bury us in our fear and inability to cope.

You are not alone if you have ever wondered if God has abandoned you. Scripture is honest about our fears and doubt and equally honest in instructing us how to not only survive, but *flourish*.

> How long, Lord? Will you forget me forever?
>> How long will you hide your face from me?
> How long must I wrestle with my thoughts
>> and day after day have sorrow in my heart?
>> How long will my enemy triumph over me?
> Look on me and answer, Lord my God.
>> Give light to my eyes, or I will sleep in death,
> and my enemy will say, "I have overcome him,"
>> and my foes will rejoice when I fall.
> But I trust in your unfailing love;
>> my heart rejoices in your salvation.
> I will sing the Lord's praise,
>> for he has been good to me. (Psalm 13)

Scripture speaks repeatedly of learning to endure and of training ourselves to walk patiently and faithfully through seasons of weariness. In a letter to the church at Corinth, Paul wrote:

Therefore we do not lose heart. Though outwardly we are wasting away, yet inwardly we are being renewed day by day. For our light and momentary troubles are achieving for us an eternal glory that far outweighs them all. So we fix our eyes not on what is seen, but on what is unseen. For what is seen is temporary, but what is unseen is eternal. (2 Corinthians 4:16–18)

Trust does not come easily in the midst of suffering.

How do we find the strength to trust, obey, and follow even when we've lost the desire to do these things? How do we move forward in faith even when it seems as if there is no good left in the universe?

DISILLUSIONMENT WITH CHRISTIANITY

Fatigue also comes as a result of disappointment with the church. Over the years I've seen many people chased away from their faith because they have been wounded by other Christians. In their resentment, they rid themselves of all that is associated with Christianity, often embittered at God Himself because (as we all know) "Christians are such hypocrites."

My own sister questioned Christianity after our favorite pastor of many years left his wife for his secretary—leaving only a note of explanation for the family to find after he'd already left. She struggled—if this pastor, this teacher, this father-of-a-friend who answered her spiritual questions as she joined them on their family vacations could abandon his family, what did that say about Christianity?

The ugly truth about Christianity is that Christians are sinners. But when those intended to bring life and encouragement appear to become the "enemy," we distance ourselves from them and end up distancing ourselves from God. In trying to rid ourselves of one problem, we can end up creating a much bigger one.

Disillusionment with the ugly side of Christianity is a real thing. Frustration at hypocrisy is a legitimate response. But abandoning the church because we have unrealistic expectations of what Christian community should be is not. In *Life Together*, Bonhoeffer explained, "By sheer grace, God will not permit us to live even for a brief period in a dream world. He does not abandon us to those rapturous experiences and lofty moods that come over us like a dream. God is not a God of the emotions but the God of truth." He added, "Only that fellowship which faces such disillusionment, with all its unhappy and ugly aspects, begins to be what it should be in God's sight, begins to grasp in faith the promise that is given to it. The sooner this shock of disillusionment comes to an individual and to a community the better for both." He concluded, "A community which cannot bear and cannot survive such a crisis, which insists upon keeping its illusion when it should be shattered, permanently loses in that moment the promise of Christian community.[5]

Are we strong enough to shatter our illusions about Christian community? Are we mature enough to extend grace and forgiveness to our brothers and sisters, even when they betray us or let us down?

JUSTICE FATIGUE

Many of my friends have been burned out by doing good. Initially filled with passion to do the work of justice, people pour themselves out zealously for the sake of the kingdom. There is a thrill that comes with giving our lives away, with being heroes and heroines doing good in the world—until we reach the point of depletion.

One reason many come crashing to a halt in their pursuit of doing what is just and right is that we are often too triumphalistic. We can get caught up in grand visions of success, transforming all of humanity through drastic strides and global movements. Asked by God to *change* the world, we may fall into unrealistic expectations of personally *fixing* the world.

Paul wrote to the church at Galatia, "Let us not become weary in doing good, for at the proper time we will reap a harvest if we do not give up. Therefore, as we have opportunity, let us do good to all people, especially to those who belong to the family of believers" (Galatians 6:9–10). There is definitely nothing to be said against the fiery zeal that comes with wanting to obey the call of God, but if we look for harvest at the beginning of summer, we are going to want to quit.

If we have realistic expectations and make justice more a part of the natural rhythm of our life, we will be on a much better trajectory to finding peace, endurance, and courage in the midst of our fatigue.

THE SOUL'S DARK NIGHT

There is another kind of fatigue Christians come upon in the life of faith. As Westerners, we may be unfamiliar with it, but the Desert Fathers understood it as a normal component of spiritual formation.[6] This kind of fatigue is what Saint John of the Cross, a sixteenth-century Spanish mystic, was referring to in his work *Dark Night of the Soul*.

Saint John understood that on our own we will never be able to attain perfect purification of our souls. It is God alone who chooses to draw some of us into what he called the crucible of reformation to be further refined in the fire of suffering. "For this reason, as we shall afterwards say, God leads into the dark night all those whom he desires to purify from all these imperfections so that he may bring them farther onward."[7]

This is the dark night, which understands fatigue as a normal process of the soul's development.

Early in the life of the believer, we are taken with the rosiness of spiritual blessing that God provides as we're learning to walk with Him. With the passing of time, as Saint John suggests, the dark night begins to loom overhead, as God purposefully distances Himself in the way that we experience His presence. C. S. Lewis echoed the same idea that God, in maturing us, makes His presence less evident after a season:

> He is prepared to do a little overriding at the beginning. He will set them off with communications of His presence which, though faint, seem great to them, with emotional sweetness, and easy conquest over temptation. But He never allows this state of affairs to last long. Sooner or later He withdraws, if not in fact, at least from their conscious experience, all those supports and incentives. He leaves the creature to stand up on its own legs—to carry out from the will alone duties which have lost all relish. It is during such trough periods, much more than during the peak periods, that it is growing into the sort of creature He wants it to be.[8]

This can be a difficult thing for us to hear. We spend a lot of time defending God, making excuses for suffering, and claiming that deliverance is right around the corner. We don't want to believe that God would ever deliberately remove stability, comfort, peace, or security from our lives, or that He would choose for us to suffer.

As trees well adapted and prepared for arid conditions find the ability to grow out of the center of a rock in the desert, we should likewise aspire to rely upon God to carry us through seasons of drought to bud and bring forth fruit despite suboptimal conditions.

When we remain faithful through periods of pain and temptation, we build endurance as a marathon runner builds endurance, by running through the ache and burn of stretching lungs and fatigued muscles.

Saint John of Avila said, "One act of thanksgiving made when things go wrong is worth a thousand when things go well."[9]

THE DEATH OF THE SONG

"Music is the universal language of mankind,"[10] said Henry Wadsworth Longfellow.

Throughout the ages worship, liturgy, and the act of giving thanks have had a rich heritage of musical expression. Since oldest antiquity, song has been used ritually as a form of emotional expression and worship for all peoples. Song and thanksgiving have always been closely connected. Take the biblical examples of Moses' sister, Miriam, singing and dancing after the crossing of the Red Sea, or of Mary, the mother of Jesus, and her famous song recorded in Luke. In it she began, "My soul glorifies the Lord," and ended with five successive declarations of what God had done for His people.

The song of thanksgiving is not an inauthentic expression of pure happiness, but one of gratitude that can be sung even in the midst of heartache. Many of the psalms are just this kind of thanksgiving song, what we call the *lament*.

The lament is an ode to the reality of heartache, a melody carried on in the plea for justice, but always followed with an assertion of God's ability to deliver. It is a melancholy tune of faith sung from the depths of suffering yet with a deeply entrenched trust in the Divine.

Out of the African-American community came rhythm and blues—a historic musical genre that embodies the very truth-telling, soul-disclosing elements of lament. Cornel West described the blues idiom as "that blue note of dissonance, of defiance."[11] Maybe that's why the blues have been so cherished for decades—because it's this dissonant and defiant resonance that captures the discordance of life's complexities and difficulties within its musical expression.

The lament gives voice to those who find themselves in the midst of trauma, who are caught in the catastrophic storm of the soul's turmoil. Sadly, within the modern evangelical church, the lament—this song of thanksgiving in suffering—seems to have met its death or demise. Our culture does not accept lament as a common component to worship. Privileged communities have hedged worship expression into narrow categories not including the agony of alienation, discrimination, slavery, and persecution.

In other words, while the African-American church was coming out of slavery and into the Jim Crow South, much of the rest of the American church was, and has remained, insulated from severe persecution and suffering. The churches of antiquity also experienced greater suffering and persecution than we typically do. The contrast between the suffering church's experience and the more insulated experience sheds light on the differences in their liturgical expression.

In fact, the lack of suffering or trial in the church can itself be a form of suffering or trial—the absence of something that can refine.

Walter Brueggemann, renowned American author and theologian, admits that the practice of lament within contemporary usage has been widely misplaced. Without lament, the people of God lose their means of voicing injustice, and worship devolves into disingenuous celebration and praise.[12]

The significance of lament lies in its relational quality. It allows for us to be initiators, and for God to respond. It also serves as a declaration of the fact that things are not as they ought to be.

Lament is about justice. "God, what will you do?"[13]

We suffer from the loss of lament because we are meant to be able to cry out to God against injustice. In Brueggemann's words, "A community of faith that negates lament soon concludes that the hard issues of justice are improper questions to pose at the throne, because the throne seems to be only a place of praise."[14]

UNDERSTANDING A THEOLOGY OF SUFFERING

Without a theology of suffering, we will assume something is wrong, broken, or out of balance whenever we face trials. We may then find ourselves wavering, frantically searching for prosperity and blessing that we believe is the Christian experience, rather than obediently moving forward in the steps of the Savior. Our comprehension of suffering as intrinsic to the life of the believer is essential if we are to find our voice among the faithful—among those who know lament.

Throughout the Psalms, we are told to sing a "new song" to the Lord.[15] As the church and as individuals, it is time that we find our song.

When we find ourselves caught in the violent grip of fatigue, suffocating in the terror of the soul's dark night, we need a song to sing. Like Paul and Silas, sitting in a damp, dark prison cell, ankles raw from heavy chains, singing loudly enough so that all the other prisoners could hear, so should we lift our voices.[16]

This need for song is really an expression of a deeper issue—our need for a richer theology of suffering.

A friend of mine, Alex Mutagubya,[17] is the founder of Transform African Ministries and pastor of the City Church in Kampala, Uganda. Speaking on the differences between the African and the American church, and on the African Christians' greater resilience in the face of trials, he said, "There is, within the African Christian community, a robust acknowledgment of spiritual warfare that informs the church's ability to endure the agony of fatigue. Even when it does not make sense, God remains God in the midst of suffering and pain."

This theology of suffering is not unique to the African church. In most of the world, the church is familiar with adversity. The prosperity of the West has sheltered us from hardship, which has led to an anemic understanding of the place of suffering in the life of believers. Songs of suffering help us endure our seasons of fatigue. Suffering should make sense to the believer.

One of the ways we come to know God is in adversity. We draw close to Jesus in suffering. The very One who calls us to follow Him was well acquainted with suffering and sorrow. "In Gethsemane the holiest of all petitioners prayed three times that a certain cup might pass from him. It did not."[18]

Paul wrote of how Jesus spoke to him of his trials, "But he said to me, 'My grace is sufficient for you, for my power is made perfect in weakness.' Therefore," Paul added, "I will boast all the more gladly about my weaknesses, so that Christ's power may rest on me. That is why, for Christ's sake, I delight in weaknesses, in insults, in hardships, in persecutions, in difficulties."

He concluded with one of the more astonishing spiritual truths of the New Testament, "For when I am weak, then I am strong."[19]

Paul had the maturity to say in the midst of difficulty that God could move and was moving. Can I also look at the challenges in my life as the grace of God? It is easy for us to see God in our blessings, but can we see God in our trials?

TRAINING TO ENDURE

It's been said that the way you train is the way you will perform. We must train ourselves for bad times as well as for good. Just as marriage covenants refer to both bad times as well as good, so our covenant with God should acknowledge the certainty of both. How we anticipate and are willing to accept pain will dictate whether we walk away or sustain faith through times of suffering.

Our expectations and preparation for trial will govern our ability to endure spiritual drought and burnout. Building a robust theology of suffering both prepares us for and acquaints us with the journey we have been called to walk.

How we train is how we perform.

How we pattern our thinking with regard to difficulty affects our response to God when difficulty comes.

In the life of faith, it is easy to tend toward either extreme optimism, a gospel of health and wealth only, or a fatalism that sees God as distant and unfeeling. A realistic understanding will accurately locate us in the middle of a story in which to suffer is to share in what it means to be human.

We have been called to follow One who understands and empathizes with suffering. Our Lord warned His disciples, "'A servant is not greater than his master.' If they persecuted me, they will persecute you also."[20]

Jesus suffered, so we should expect to suffer. We should expect it, but we should also begin to rebuild a proper theology of suffering within our confessions of faith. We need to strengthen our trust that, although we will undoubtedly meet adversity and pain on His account, He is also the one who has overcome the world and in whom we have life.

As Corrie ten Boom, the famed Dutch Christian whose family hid Jews from the Nazis during World War II, once said, "joy runs deeper than despair."[21]

I waited patiently for the Lord; he turned to me and heard my cry.
—Psalm 40:1

BLESSING COME LATE

"God bless us, every one!"[1]
—CHARLES DICKENS, *A CHRISTMAS CAROL*

One of the problems of the dark night of the soul is that it can produce a certain melancholy tone in our relationship with God if we're unable to balance it with a biblical sense of God's blessings and provision.

Along these lines, have you ever considered that our confidence in the One to whom we are praying can be directly proportional to the degree of specificity in our prayers and belief in the personal nature of our relationship with God?

My wife, Tamara, came from a culture in which serious Christians did not ask God for anything desired that did not clearly fall into the "necessities" category. Her understanding of the function of prayer was limited to an acknowledgment or submission to "Thy will be done," which, from her perspective, did not include anything personal or desirable.

As our wedding was fast approaching, we were looking for an apartment to rent in Los Angeles that was both affordable and safe, but I wanted more; I wanted it to be a place to make a home, for her to love it, and to have a clear sense of God's leading in finding the right place.

We agreed it was something we would pray for, but when I asked Tamara to make a list of all the things she would want in an apartment and to put that list on paper so we could pray specifically, she adamantly refused. She did not believe that Christians had any place asking God for more than they absolutely needed.

I persisted with my request and, begrudgingly, she made the list. Did I ever pray! I didn't care so much about the apartment, but that my soon-to-be wife would experience the goodness and closeness of a loving Father who tenderly hears our prayers, cares, and delights to give good gifts to His children in answer to specific requests.

We all long for confirmation that God is listening. But often we are praying prayers that are so vague we wouldn't notice if God answered them or not. Or, we find ourselves so afraid that God isn't going to answer that we just don't ask for anything at all.

In conversations about prayer, we have probably either said or heard something like, "God isn't Santa Claus." This is true. He does not exist to serve all our needs, but sometimes we land on the opposite extreme: we think He does not care about our requests at all.

I was passionate about not wanting this for Tamara.

I wanted her to understand just how much God desires to bless His children. I wanted her to know that prayer didn't have to be resigned or fatalistic, and neither did her relationship with Him.

One day, as we were continuing our apartment search, I was praying hard while driving on La Mirada Boulevard, a road I drove every day for nearly seven years, when I looked up and saw a sign for a small apartment complex I had never before noticed. It was a little village of apartments tucked away from the street down a narrow driveway.

I got out and talked to the manager. She told me about an apartment that was open within our price range. There was a long waiting list, as was common for apartments in the greater Los Angeles area back then, but she smiled and, for whatever reason, said she'd move us up to the front of the list.

The unit required refurbishing because the previous tenants, two brothers who were smokers, had lived there for twenty years. It needed new carpet, fresh paint, and even updated appliances, but all of this would be ready the week before our wedding.

That apartment answered every single item on the list, and even, as Tamara later sheepishly confessed, the few items she really wanted but had refused to add to the list, feeling they were over-the-top.

Tamara and I prayed a specific prayer that God could answer specifically, and it changed the course of our lives. It was a blessing to me and it was a profound experience of God's fatherly goodness to Tamara. Since then, we have worked hard to pray about as much as we can and try to place as many choices as we can before Him.

Many prayers I pray and have prayed since the apartment story have gone unanswered or unfulfilled, but I believe if we do not pray with specificity—actually boil it down or put it in writing—it may be difficult to notice if and when God answers.

Although God does not exist to give us what we want when we want it, He has expressed a desire to give the good things we need when we're walking with Him. It gives Him pleasure to bestow them on us.

A CORDIAL FOR HEALING (GIFTS FOR OUR CALLING)

Often God blesses us by giving us what He knows we need to live effectively and fulfill the calling He has for us. Both Lewis and Tolkien have interesting ways of expressing this in their two famous book series, The Chronicles of Narnia and The Lord of the Rings.

In *The Lion, the Witch and the Wardrobe*, Father Christmas meets the Pevensie children and provides them with the items necessary to carry out their calling as kings and queens of Narnia: a sword for Peter, a bow and arrows for Susan, a bottle of healing cordial for Lucy.[2] As you might guess, each uses his or her gift wisely and at critical points in their subsequent battles.

Their brother Edmund isn't there, because he has been taken in by the charm of the evil White Witch. What gift does he receive from her? Candy. This is a gift that consists of momentary pleasure, instant gratification, and nothing that will actually prepare him for his role as a future king. Because of his decision to leave his siblings and follow his own desires, Edmund has to wait much longer to receive his true gifts.

In *The Fellowship of the Ring*, the elven queen, Galadriel, provides to Aragorn a sheath for his great sword, to Legolas a bow, to Sam a box of elven earth for his garden, to Gimli a lock of her hair to remind him of his reconciliation with the elves, and to Frodo a vial of starlight to keep him safe in the darkness of Mordor. All of these items had great significance and lasting value, particularly in the eyes of the gifted.

Both Lewis and Tolkien had a rich theology of blessing. They illustrated well that the best gifts are not luxury items or "cotton candy" pleasures, but rather the specific items we need to succeed in our calling. The best gifts equip us to accomplish the tasks and live the lives that God has for us.

It is an interesting question . . . If I looked for God's hand of blessing set in my context, what would He give me? Would it be wisdom for parenting? Would it be endurance to bear up under stress? Would it be patience or grace for the day's interruptions?

What would God give you that would enable or enhance your success in ministry, family, or His calling on your life?

Additionally, Jesus tells us an astounding truth: the more we use the gifts God has already given us, the more gifts He will give.

In Matthew 25, Jesus tells the parable of the talents (an ancient form of currency). In this parable, before a rich man goes on a long journey, he entrusts three of his servants with money. He gives one servant five talents, another two talents, and the last servant one talent.

While their master is gone, the first two servants invest the money and double what he had entrusted to them. The last servant buries the money in the ground, knowing that the master will demand it when he returns.

When the master returns, he is pleased with the first two servants, who multiplied their monies, but he is furious with the last servant, who buried his one talent. He was outraged that the servant didn't even bother to do the bare minimum with the money—put it in the bank, where it would earn interest. He takes away the one talent and gives it to the servant who has ten. "Whoever has will be given more, and they will have an abundance. Whoever does not have, even what they have will be taken from them" (Matthew 13:12).

He who has much will be given more—because that servant is using it well, or in other words, using it for the kingdom, justice, and will of God in this world.

Stewardship begets blessing.

Just as the behavior of children and employees either earns or forfeits trust and responsibility, our stewardship of God's gifts will elicit His rewards or His disappointment. Being faithful leads to blessing (and blessings take many forms).

Faithfulness with what we have is one of the surest ways to experience a greater blessing from God.

Picture a classroom of second graders for a moment. Imagine there's a difficult child bullying his fellow students and disrespecting the teacher. I cannot affirm that child. Even if I know his story, that he came from a troubled home, and want to comfort and encourage him, there is nothing *in his behavior* that I could encourage. I could love, I could forgive, I could listen, but I could not affirm the behavior. Affirmation, after all, is a form of encouragement.

Sometimes I think God is desperately waiting for us to give Him one small indication of obedience so He can pour out His full measure of affirmation, encouragement, and blessing. A father cannot encourage a wrong heart, but delights in affirming whatever good he can. In time, the nurturing of small acts of obedience gives rise to the fullness of character and blessing.

A SLOW TRAIN COMING

One of the hardest things about prayer is that it can go unanswered for so long. It is difficult for me to accept the truth that God has a different view of time than I do—that He has a different sense of urgency than I do. For, as Peter wrote (quoting the Psalms), "with the Lord a day is like a thousand years, and a thousand years are like a day."[3]

What this means is that God is more patient than I am in some areas (for example, how perfect I think my life should be right now) and more earnest than I in other areas (for example, how important it is for me to pursue justice and compassion for the orphan, the widow, and the immigrant).

The leadership examples we see in the Old Testament seem to show that God is not always in a hurry to bring His children into their calling.

Earlier in this book we looked at the account of Abraham and Isaac. The name Isaac means "he laughs," which has both a positive and a negative connotation. In the negative, Abraham's wife, Sarah, laughed a bit sarcastically when she overheard God's messengers telling Abraham they would have a son. She didn't believe the promise.

But in Genesis 21:6 she gave another reason for naming him Isaac: "God has brought me laughter, and everyone who hears about this will laugh with me." The laughter that began as a scoff of disbelief became a joyful celebration—but it was not until many years down the road that the blessing was fully realized.

After Moses received his calling to lead the children of Israel, he was forced to flee from Egypt to the country of Midian, where he tended sheep for decades. He was in the desert so long that he despaired of receiving God's blessing on the calling he had received many years earlier.

When God finally appeared in a burning bush to call Moses into leadership (Exodus 3), Moses no longer wanted the calling: "Who am I that I should go to Pharaoh and bring the Israelites out of Egypt?" (v. 11).

God's blessing outlasted Moses' desire to be blessed.

The prophet Samuel anointed David as king when he was only a boy, but he had to live as a public enemy for years, running for his life. It was after years of hiding out in caves, eating whatever he and his men could scrape together, and being isolated from the people he loved that God saw fit to bring him to the throne.

The blessing of God often looks different than we think it ought to look and may be on a very different timetable. For one thing, it is often a spiritual blessing more than a material one. Second, as with David, Moses, and Abraham, there is a place in time when the blessing is announced, but the ramifications of that blessing evolve across a lifetime.

We tend to deeply inquire and ask, "God, will You bless me?" That being so, I think it is interesting that the first words in the Psalms are "Blessed is the one . . ." The answer to how God could or might bless us is less a secret than we think. It also turns out to be more of a process than we would wish.

Nothing expresses God's system and pattern of blessing more concisely and vividly, I believe, than the entirety of that first psalm.

> Blessed is the one
>> who does not walk in step with the wicked
>> or stand in the way that sinners take
>> or sit in the company of mockers,
>> but whose delight is in the law of the LORD,
>> and who meditates on his law day and night.
>> That person is like a tree planted by streams of water,
>> which yields its fruit in season
>> and whose leaf does not wither—
>> whatever they do prospers. (vv. 1–3)

In this psalm, agriculture is used as a metaphor for a flourishing person. Imagine how an agrarian people, well acquainted with crops and with the seasons of tilling, planting, tending, and harvesting, would hear the words of Psalm 1. They would have a very specific picture of a life that "yields its fruit in season."

In this industrial age, in which we can obtain strawberries from the market during any month of the year, we have a mind-set of immediacy. We often don't think of the seasonal cycle of agriculture, of wisdom through age, or of maturation through growth. When we hear the word *blessing*, we are likely to anticipate immediate results.

Fruit, however, does not show up ready-made at the grocery store—it is the product of a long, slow process (it is, after all, called *produce*).

Ancient cultures—up to the time when Psalm 1 was written—saw life as cyclical, and built their lives around the unending turn of the seasons. The Israelites were the first (because of God's revelation to them) to begin to understand that time had a beginning, a forward progress, a continuing purpose. This sense of time has been acknowledged as one of the gifts that Jewish culture offered to humanity.[4] But because they depended on agriculture, their view of time was balanced by their understanding of repeating seasons, even in a linear progression.

The Greeks emphasized the linear nature of time, and the Romans produced calendars meant to remain accurate throughout the passing centuries. As a result, unless you are a farmer or rancher, we tend to see time almost exclusively in linear terms. In our paradigm, one event leads to another, which leads to another, and we do our best to keep all of the events on a continually rising trajectory.

For the Israelite, seasons of growth, harvest, decay, hibernation, rain, snow, and sunshine were natural patterns in the cycle of life. They would have understood that these seasons were very much out of man's control, that the best they could do was submit to the conditions and processes created by the Lord to produce fruit. They knew that they could and should trust and wait on the One who created the earth and provided the rain in its season.

As we read Scripture, we see that God's blessing on the obedience of His people often follows far behind the actual act of obedience. Isn't this also how we experience life as well? Does not the fruit of education or music lessons as a child follow long after the actual spelling tests and hours practicing guitar? This is especially true of God's gifts, which often take the form of skills or individual talents, and which need to be honed and grown through use before they are ready to yield final results. Money is far from the only investment that grows in value over long periods of time.

Likewise, much of God's blessing is a slow train coming.

"Blessing come late" is a phrase I use to describe how we should perceive the promise of blessing made in Scripture not as an immediate, sequential process. Instead, blessing often grows over a long period of time, is stored up until the end of our lives, or in extreme cases, as with the lives of the martyrs, is held in reserve until after we die.

THE BLESSING WE CAN'T SEE

One of the distinctions we must make is that there is a difference between momentary blessings and blessed lives, which grow slowly over time. All good things originate from God, and everyone experiences instances of blessing, but not all of us experience the fullness of a blessed life born out of a long obedience to God.

Ancient philosophers talked about *the good, the true, and the beautiful,* as the object of our pursuits leading to the ultimate aim of *the flourishing of the soul.* Wisdom literature and proverbial sayings have much to say about this, and little affirmation for our inclination to instant gratification.

Joy results from obedience. The more we learn to walk with God and, accordingly, the more we experience closeness with God, the more familiar we become with obedience as a source of joy itself. It's not that God is always going to reward us with gifts and pleasure because we've obeyed so well; instead, we may begin to find our joy in obedience.

A helpful distinction might be between the kinds of grace we experience as Christians. The English word *grace* means "God's favor or help," and derives from the Latin *gratia*—meaning "favor, esteem, regard; pleasing quality, good will, gratitude."[5]

Saving grace, what we typically think about when talking about God's grace, is the "unmerited favor" or blessing we receive because of Jesus' death on the cross. We don't work for this grace and can't earn it. As Paul said, "For it is by grace you have been saved, through faith—and this is not from yourselves, it is the gift of God—not by works, so that no one can boast" (Ephesians 2:8–9).

There is another kind of grace, however. This grace is sustaining grace, or blessing along the way. It doesn't connote salvation, but divine favor. The significant difference is that blessings along the way can be a result of our leaning into our calling and walking by faith.

This is why Paul concluded his short section in Ephesians 2 on being made alive in Christ with this thought: "For we are God's handiwork, created in Christ Jesus to do good works, which God prepared in advance for us to do" (v. 10).

I did not do anything to become Ken Wytsma, son of John and Bonnie, just as I can't do anything to be born again into the kingdom and family of God. But, just as obedience and faithfulness in the Wytsma household while growing up brought blessing and favor, so, too, do obedience and faith create the conditions where God can bless or show favor in my life now.

Joy comes from obedience because in it we experience living the call God has for us. We get to do the work He created for us, and growing into a deeper walk of faith and trust in Him.

If we do not make the distinction between saving grace and sustaining grace, we end up removing obedience from the table without knowing where to place it. Obedience is a necessary piece in our theological puzzle, an essential cog in the engine of our Christian walk of faith.

CAUGHT IN THE MIDDLE

The distinction between saving grace and sustaining grace has severe implications for people who ride the fence and sit in the middle between worldly living and Christian living. They think they have enough of God, but have found ways to avoid the Christian walk or obedience while trying to hold on to a fair measure of the world. It doesn't work. I find the people caught in the middle to be the most miserable, as they often have neither the blessings of God nor the benefits of the world.

I have a huge heart for people still caught in this category. It is one of the reasons why I believe clear thinking in the church is necessary—as the outcomes of what many call *cheap grace*[6] (grace without cost, without walking by faith, and without obedience) are so destructive to so many people hungry for blessing.

The leap of faith about which Kierkegaard talked—moving forward and trusting that obedience is the path of truth and blessing (even if we can't see it)—truly is what it means to be Christian. As Jesus simply said, "Come, and follow Me."

I have a friend who has struggled for a long time with wanting God in his life. The trouble is, he is not willing to do anything about it. He wants God and His blessing, but he also wants his own idea of happiness, which for him means living a worldly life.

He calls just about every time he hits rock bottom, feels depressed, and is desperate to get his life in order. As the pattern plays out, I will give the same advice I always do—jump wholeheartedly into following and obeying God, and do it for the long haul. He typically responds by using spiritual-sounding language to consider what I am saying; but after two days or maybe a week, he veers off, jumps into another illicit relationship, and finds himself right back where he started. He always goes for the quick fix or the worldly way of relieving the pain and tension.

It breaks my heart.

We don't earn blessing from God, but we can submit to the conditions for blessing. Blessing arises from obedience like the blossom growing on the rosebush, the rain falling from the cloud, the laugh exploding from a tickle, the smile after a joke, the warmth from a hug.

Obedience and blessing go together—not as a transaction or religious gimmick, but naturally and organically. Obedience *is* the seed of blessing.

THE LOGIC OF WASHING IN DIRTY RIVERS

Long ago, there lived a man named Naaman. Naaman, the commander of the Syrian army, was afflicted with leprosy. The event unfolds in 2 Kings

5 as one of Naaman's servants tells him about a prophet in Israel named Elisha, who could heal his disease. Naaman goes to the Syrian king and asks for permission to seek out this healer, and the king sends him to Israel.

When Naaman arrives at Elisha's house, rather than welcoming the powerful Syrian leader into his home, Elisha sends a messenger saying simply: "Wash seven times in the Jordan River, and you'll be clean."

Naaman reacts strongly:

> But Naaman went away angry and said, "I thought that he would surely come out to me and stand and call on the name of the LORD his God, wave his hand over the spot and cure me of my leprosy. Are not Abana and Pharpar, the rivers of Damascus, better than all the waters of Israel? Couldn't I wash in them and be cleansed?" (vv. 11–12)

The Jordan River is small and shallow, averaging between two and ten feet deep in many places during dry seasons, and can also be clouded with silt. Naaman wasn't impressed, so he headed back to Syria, offended by Elisha's suggestion and dismissive treatment. But his servants stopped him: "If the prophet had told you to do some great thing, would you not have done it?" (v. 13)

Recognizing their wisdom, Naaman decided to do what Elisha instructed. He bathed in the Jordan seven times and was healed.

If Naaman had remained hung up on the fact that the Jordan River was dirty, that Elisha didn't honor his position, or that the instructions were beneath him, he would have missed out on the blessing.

Like Naaman, we often think we have a better idea of how God's blessing in our lives should work—quicker, easier, cleaner, more straightforward. In short, we want God's blessing on our terms rather than His. We don't want to get dirty.

We have a specific time when we would like blessing to show up, we don't want to be embarrassed, and we don't want to lose any of our perceived dignity. Instead of yielding, we resist and keep searching.

We will take the blessing, but only on our terms.

Somehow, if we are to understand faith correctly, we need to recover a more accurate and biblically grounded account of what it means to be blessed and how that comes about.

God does promise blessing, and it is possible to experience a blessed life. The path, however, is of necessity on His terms.

Over time, trust and obedience are how God chooses to shape us into the right kind of people with the right kinds of desires—people able to experience the true happiness, contentment, and joy He desires for us. All other specific blessings God chooses to bestow on us along the way or down the road are merely the reflections of a Father's heart, a Father who cares for His children and delights to give them good gifts.

Every good and perfect gift is from above, coming
down from the Father of the heavenly lights, who
does not change like shifting shadows.
—JAMES 1:17

16

BETWEEN THE GARDENS

Life must be lived forward, but can only be understood backward.[1]
—SØREN KIERKEGAARD

One of my favorite authors is Blaise Pascal, the brilliant mathematician, prolific inventor, clear thinker, and Christian apologist. Pascal, who lived between 1623 and 1662, died unexpectedly at the age of thirty-nine, before he could publish his thoughts on Christianity and religion, but his journals were published as the book *Pensees* (Thoughts), which has been a world classic for hundreds of years. I've always thought it amazing and inspiring that Pascal was so insightful that his private notes and incomplete thoughts were published after he died.

One of his thought experiments has become known as Pascal's Wager.

Pascal is regarded as the founder of probability theory, and Pascal's Wager is essentially an argument for belief in God in the form of a risk-rewards analysis. The point is that if you bet that God doesn't exist and you lose, you lose everything (heaven, eternal life). If, on the other hand, you bet on God existing and lose, you lose nothing. It's a simple win-win argument.

In other words, Pascal envisioned that if we live as though God doesn't exist, we get to live a brief life of earthly pleasure,[2] and we stand to either lose eternal happiness (if we're wrong) or simply die and cease to exist if we're right that God doesn't exist.

Rather, if we live a life of faith in God, Pascal believed we stand to either gain an eternity of happiness (on the one hand) or simply live a good life here and then die (on the other hand). Pascal's Wager seeks to prove that disbelief in God entails low reward and high risk and that belief in God, on the contrary, entails high reward and low risk.

Pascal sees the choice to believe in God as a win-win, whether He actually exists or not.

But there are circumstances in which aspects of this argument are not so applicable.

In the wager, the cost (in this life) of believing in God is deemed to be negligible. We can certainly think of cultures in which belief in God generally—or following Christ in particular—did not itself entail any exposure to persecution or risk and did not involve any suffering beyond the normal human experience. Pascal's culture may have been like that, and cultures like it have existed throughout much of America's brief history.

But in many other cultures there has been a significant cost associated with belief—a cost to health, life, liberty, and peace. This was certainly the case in the early church, and remains the case in many parts of the world right up to the present. It is these cultures—not Pascal's or Christian America's—that are in line with the depictions by Jesus and the writers of the New Testament of what it means to follow Christ. Jesus promised pain, suffering, and death. Paul declared in 1 Corinthians 15 that if Jesus didn't rise from the dead—if the core of Christianity isn't true—then Christians are to be the most pitied of all people, because their gamble, in a very literal sense, was a bad choice.

I think the tension between Pascal's Wager and some of the sober and straightforward teachings in the New Testament surface the real tension regarding the stakes of what it means to go *all in*. Going all in with our belief in God and our commitment to trust and obey is to take Kierkegaard's leap of faith and hold nothing in reserve. It is to be a Christian who lives with faith in the resurrection of Jesus Christ, or, as Wendell Berry put it in a poem he wrote, to "practice resurrection."[3]

God *wants* us to live by faith and experience Him, and He's made it possible for us to do exactly that. The just walk by faith, not by sight. Most of us experience, to some degree, the messiness of life and the mystery of God. These things are not distinct from faith: faith emerges from a perspective of things hoped for but not yet seen. We are caught in the vicissitudes of life, and the only way forward is through the difficult decisions to obey and trust God's promises.

Faith is a beautifully awkward reality.

When we understand it correctly, the question is less what people typically ask about life, "What have I been doing wrong?" but rather a more hopeful one, "How can I start living by faith and experiencing God?"

THE MESSY MIDDLE

The day after Christmas in 2004, a tsunami ravaged the shores of many Asian countries and reached as far as the beaches on the eastern coast of Africa. Many of us will never forget the images and the magnitude of suffering that occurred that day, leaving 150,000 dead and millions without homes in eleven countries.[4]

The following Sunday, I gave a sermon I called "Between the Gardens." The central theme was that we live between the garden of Eden and the gardens of Zion and the New Jerusalem described in the book of Revelation. Our season is the messy middle. We aspire to, rather than live in, utopia.

In act 2 of Shakespeare's *The Tempest*, Antonio says to Sebastian, "What's past is prologue." I find that a fitting picture for the Christian perspective on the idea that we have *now* many of the blessings, but *not yet* all of what is to come. What's past—the trials, the difficulties, the struggles—are really just the beginning. They are the prologue. They are what the author writes to set the stage for the act to come.

In Scripture, this same idea is seen in Joseph's summation of the long, drawn-out struggles of his life: "You intended to harm me, but God intended it for good" (Genesis 50:20). It is seen in Job's humility, recognizing a God bigger, grander, and wiser than his own questions and frustrations. It is the resurrection and the new covenant, which charts a radically new course and opens up a new chapter following all that had come before. What's past is prologue.

In the current chapter of the story, much of what we are called to is suffering. We know pain. We experience brokenness. We endure heartache, shame, and loss. Like Shakespeare's Antonio, however, we can see this suffering as simply setting the scene for the really great stuff. We are living the prologue, and the final drama still dances on the horizon. We know it by intuition. We sense it by desire. We reach for it by necessity.

The tensions of this broken world come to the surface most dramatically in disasters and tragedies. Cheap answers and religious quick fixes don't really work. Instead they leave us wanting something solid and hoping to find bedrock on which to build the foundation of our lives. Our hope can't simply be in the fixing of present circumstances; instead, it has to be grounded in the future garden—when all is made right.

If we talk about living by faith, a large part must seek its ultimate resolution in the promised consummation, not in this life of struggle. Beauty *does* come from ashes, darkness *does* turn to light; and when we, as strangers here, arrive at our heavenly home, what's past will have been only the prologue.

GETHSEMANE

The experience of Jesus in the Garden of Gethsemane—the garden between Eden and Zion—epitomizes the paradoxical nature of His entire earthly life.[5] The One who made and sustains the whole universe placed Himself in a position to face excruciating, humiliating torture and death. The uniquely sinless man was about to allow the sins of all humanity to be placed upon

Him. The One who enjoyed unbroken, eternal community with the Father was about to experience separation from Him.

But then, Jesus' whole life was lived from the bottom up. The story of Jesus is full of paradox.

Though He was the most powerful man ever to live, Jesus exemplified humility.

Though He was the most loving of all men, Jesus endured the great depths of human hatred.

Though He was a dynamic leader, Jesus washed His followers' feet, coming not to be served but to serve.

Though He had the purest and greatest calling and mission in life, Jesus endured the greatest obstacles and apparent defeats en route to accomplishing that mission.

Though He was the one whom the Father would use to redeem the world, Jesus had to allow that world to first crush Him.

VISION

One of the things the bottom-up ministry of Jesus teaches us is the importance of holding our goals and our dreams loosely. From a human, rational standpoint, I really do believe in creating goals, maps, and visions for the areas of our life. Focused effort and energy is an unbelievably powerful way to make sure to accomplish what you've set out to do. But we must be willing to allow the Holy Spirit permission to change our direction at any time.

Perhaps the best way to understand this is by examining the way God led Israel in the desert. It was God, rather than the people's immediate feelings or needs, that dictated their course. As they walked during the day, God used clouds to lead the Israelites, and by night, a pillar of fire. When the clouds or the fire stopped, the people stopped and set up the tabernacle. When the clouds or fire moved, they moved.

Is that not the epitome of living and walking by faith? We learn two things from this. The first is that God leads. The second is that somehow and in some way His leading is going to be visible enough for us to have confidence in it, even if we don't have certainty about where He's taking us.

When we walk in faith, we have a sense of the bigness of our God, but not always knowledge about where life is going, or where He is taking us. May we always hold our plans loosely and with open hands. May we sacrifice our own agendas and simply follow.

> Unless the LORD builds the house,
>   its builders labor in vain.
> Unless the LORD watches over the city,
>   the watchmen stand guard in vain. (Psalm 127:1)

Where your heart is, there your treasure is also. Where your desire is strongest, there your greatest resources and energy will be spent. Our paradigms shape our pursuits. Desires determine decisions and direction.

Change your priorities and you change yourself.

ENDURANCE

Gardening in Central Oregon is challenging. Because of the relatively short growing season, it is a struggle to produce hot-weather crops, like tomatoes or melons. In addition, we often seem to go straight from winter to summer, with not much of a spring in between.

Under these conditions, growing cool-weather salad greens—spinach, arugula, and lettuce—is most effective. If you plant seeds of these crops in late September (preferably in a cold frame), they will germinate and sprout before the onset of winter. The cold will then cause them to go dormant long before the leaves are large enough to harvest. But then, with the first intimations of returning warmth—even in February or early March—these seedlings will begin to flourish, to become what they were meant to become. Having endured a cold season that made growth impossible, they have become strengthened and positioned for the rapid fulfillment of the role for which they were designed.

Isn't this a picture of our lives?

Our own seasons of dormancy can be used by God to strengthen our roots. Maybe the messy parts of our lives are not mere anomalies but are actually intended by God as part of our growth and maturity. We need to avoid obsessing about the challenges and obstacles we will surely face and focus instead on the opportunities for cultivation these challenges may present.

Life is too precious to waste any season of it.

Much of this life comes down to endurance. We may be called upon to endure fatigue, anxiety, despair, confusion, heartache, disappointment. We may need to endure good people who let us down or bad people who sabotage our goals or even our reputations. We may have to endure through unanswered questions and sleepless nights.

From Abraham and his roundabout travels, to Moses in the desert, to David in a lonely cave, running for his life, to John the Baptist in a prison, to Mary being visited in a dream about an unconsummated pregnancy, to Jesus in a lonely garden in solitude, it seems that the calling of God or His movement in the lives of His people often goes hand in hand with sleepless nights.

The life of faith may mean keeping our feet moving when we don't know where, doing when we don't know how, and hoping when we don't know why. When we take Kierkegaard's leap of faith, we find the beautifully awkward resolution to the messiness of life, the mystery of God, and the challenge of authentic spirituality.

In such a life, between the gardens, we need to be able to follow Henri Nouwen's advice—to live the questions. Or, put another way, to wait on the Lord, to pray our pain, and to accept confusion as part of human experience.

GOD COME NEAR

Often, I think, the main problem in Christianity is that the blind so often seem to lead the blind. Of course we are supposed to seek wise counsel from trusted advisors, but that is not supposed to replace the One whom we should be seeking, who has the best counsel and the last word. God has promised that if we seek Him, we will find Him.

> But if from there you seek the LORD your God, you will find him if you seek him with all your heart and with all your soul. (Deuteronomy 4:29)

> I [wisdom] love those who love me,
>   and those who seek me find me. (Proverbs 8:17)

> You will seek me and find me when you seek me with all your heart. (Jeremiah 29:13)

> Let us acknowledge the LORD;
>   let us press on to acknowledge him.
>   As surely as the sun rises,
>   he will appear;
>   he will come to us like the winter rains,
>   like the spring rains that water the earth. (Hosea 6:3)

> Ask and it will be given to you; seek and you will find; knock and the door will be opened to you. For everyone who asks receives; the one who seeks finds; and to the one who knocks, the door will be opened. (Matthew 7:7–8)

> God did this so that they would seek him and perhaps reach out for him and find him, though he is not far from any one of us. (Acts 17:27)

> Come near to God and he will come near to you. (James 4:8)

This is the joy we have in God—He is a God come near. Our joy can extend beyond ourselves. Our wandering and searching has a resolution.

THE SHADOW-LANDS

This concept of living "between the gardens" was characterized by C. S. Lewis as living in the "Shadow-lands"—the lands on the edge of heaven that are less real, less solid, and less permanent than heaven itself.

In 2005 I backpacked through Europe with my friend Jon Lemke to study Lewis, World War II history, and the Reformation. While in Oxford we had a chance to walk the university grounds and meet with Walter Hooper, a longtime literary executor of the C. S. Lewis estate.

Lewis had an amazing ability to articulate deep truths through uncanny metaphor and description, but he also lived a very human life. I see in Lewis the picture of a sinner/saint, someone who dealt with pain, world wars, loneliness, heartbreak, loss, and, at times, rejection. Lewis was able to write magically about the Shadow-lands while the same themes were being etched deep into his own life.

At one of the entrances to a gentle, mile-long footpath along a stream behind Oxford's Magdalen College, named after essayist Joseph Addison (1672–1719), there is a poem by C. S. Lewis cast in a semicircular plaque of bronze.

The poem is about Addison's Walk, which Lewis frequently walked with students and friends, and it was on Addison's Walk that Lewis had a conversation with J. R. R. Tolkien that led to his conversion to Christianity.

The poem is on the hope of breaking forth and is a fitting end to our story:

What the Bird Said Early in the Year

I heard in Addison's Walk a bird sing clear:
This year the summer will come true. This year. This year.
Winds will not strip the blossom from the apple trees
this year, nor want of rain destroy the peas.

This year time's nature will no more defeat you,
nor all the promised moments in their passing cheat you.
This time they will not lead you round and back
to autumn, one year older, by the well-worn track.
This year, this year, as all these flowers foretell,
we shall escape the circle and undo the spell.
Often deceived, yet open once again your heart,
Quick, quick, quick, quick!—the gates are drawn apart.

—C. S. Lewis, 1898–1963

ACKNOWLEDGMENTS

I want to thank all those who have been patient with me as I have tried to understand and live the paradox of faith.

To my wife, Tamara, and my daughters, Mary Joy, Esther, Sara, and Ashlin. Your grace and love in our home is my joy.

To Mom and Dad—thank you for shaping me into who I am.

To my sister, Laura, for your ongoing support and encouragement.

To Rick Gerhardt and Ben Larson for extensive writing and editorial assistance on the manuscript.

To Emily Hill and Tabitha Sikich—thank you for your immense contributions to the manuscript and support throughout this project.

To Justin Kron who helped with writing and research on Nazareth.

To Don Dunscomb, Melissa Wuske, Gerry Breshears, Pat Kent, Linda Van Voorst, Gretchen Radomski, Peter Watts, Dawn Gerhardt, Jasper Gerhardt, Pam Johnson, Laura Wytsma, Martita Marx, Caitlin Querio, Aaron Pratt, Brandi Nichols, Sam Adams, David Miller, Matt Bane, and

Tyler Lacoma, who helped with reading, feedback, and creative contributions in making this book better than I could have on my own.

To Don Jacobson, Ed Underwood, and Matt Smith for the encouragement to write.

To the Antioch community for keeping me sane with regard to Christianity and what authenticity looks like.

To Kilns College: Melissa McCreery, Mike Caba, Rick Gerhardt, Sam Adams, and the many others, for the dreams we have and the beautiful future you are creating for a community of faith, justice, and learning in Bend, Oregon.

To the folks at Thomas Nelson Publishers for all the time and energy invested in me and this project.

NOTES

EPIGRAPH

1. G. K. Chesterton, *Heretics* (Rockville, MD: Serenity, 2009), 116.

CHAPTER 1

1. Largely attributed to George MacDonald. Martin H. Manser, *The Westminster Collection of Christian Quotes* (Louisville: Westminster John Knox, 2001), 2.
2. "The Walls of Jericho," *NIV Archaeological Study Bible* (Grand Rapids: Zondervan, 2003), 312.
3. Thomas Brisco, *Holman Bible Atlas* (Nashville: Broadman & Holman, 1998), 18, 34.
4. Deut. 34:3, Judg. 3:13 KJV.
5. "From Jerusalem to Jericho," Bible Resource Center, American Bible Society, bibleresources.americanbible.org, accessed December 3, 2013.
6. Jerome F. D. Creach, *Joshua* (Louisville: John Knox Press, 2003), 61.
7. Roy Liran and Ran Barkai, "Casting a Shadow on Neolithic Jericho," *Antiquity* 85, no. 327 (March 2011), http://antiquity.ac.uk/projgall/barkai327/.
8. 2 Sam. 10.

NOTES

9. Matt. 20:29–34; Mark 10:46–52; Luke 18:35–43.
10. Luke 19:1–10.
11. For those not familiar with this story, it makes up a big part of the Old Testament books of Exodus and Joshua.
12. Throughout the Old Testament, the ark is the symbol of God's presence with His people, and is so closely associated with God Himself that the people were commanded to keep their distance from it because of his holiness present with the symbol. Marten H. Woudstra, *The Book of Joshua* (Grand Rapids: Eerdmans, 1981), 80.
13. Josh. 4.
14. Josh. 5:13–15.
15. Josh. 6.
16. Josh. 7:1.
17. The original Hebrew word for Achan's disobedience literally means he "broke faith." His actions betrayed his lack of trust in God. Woudstra, *The Book of Joshua*, 120.
18. Ex. 20:1–7.
19. Bruce Wilkinson and Kenneth Boa, *The Wilkinson and Boa Bible Handbook* (Nashville: Thomas Nelson, 2002), 52.

CHAPTER 2

1. William Shakespeare, *Macbeth*, act 4, scene 3.
2. N.p.: Other Press, 2010.
3. Henri J. M. Nouwen, *Spiritual Direction: Wisdom for the Long Walk of Faith* (New York: HarperCollins, 2006), 4.

CHAPTER 3

1. Soren Kierkegaard, *Works of Love* (New York: Harper and Row Publishers, 1962), 42.
2. Soren Kierkegaard, *Concluding Unscientific Postscript to Philosophical Fragments* (Princeton: Princeton University Press, 1992), 430.

CHAPTER 4

1. Brother Lawrence, *The Practice of the Presence of God and the Spiritual Maxims* (n.p.: Benton, 2013), 25.
2. Matt. 6:5–6.
3. 1 Thess. 5:17 KJV; 2 Cor. 13:14.
4. Phil. 4:6; Luke 18:1–8.
5. Matt. 6:7–8.

198

6. Heb. 4:16 KJV; Rom. 8:15.

7. Rom. 8:14–16; John 15:14–15.

8. Ex. 3:6; Isa. 6:5 KJV.

9. David Winter, *Closer than a Brother* (London: Holder and Stoughton, 1971), 6.

10. 1 Kings 19:11–13.

11. Ps. 19:14; emphasis added; Phil. 4:8.

CHAPTER 5

1. "Nicholas Wolterstorff on Justice, Art, Love & Human Flourishing," an interview with Nicholas Wolterstorff, which can be found on my blog, at http://kenwytsma.com/2013/12/02/nicholas-wolterstorff-on-justice-art-love-human-flourishing/.

2. The story of the Universal Declaration of Human Rights is powerfully told by Mary Ann Glendon in a book appropriately titled *A World Made New* (New York: Random House, 2001).

3. 2 Cor. 5:11–21, (esp. vv. 18–20).

4. "Nicholas Wolterstorff on Justice, Art, Love & Human Flourishing."

5. For the philosopher, substances need not be material entities.

6. The best treatment of these issues I know of is *Welcoming the Stranger*, by my friends Matthew Soerens and Jenny Hwang (Downers Grove, IL: InterVarsity Press, 2009).

7. See Matthew 26:40.

8. Hab. 2:4 KJV; Rom. 1:17 KJV; Heb. 10:38 KJV. As discussed earlier, several modern English translations wrongly choose the word *righteous* here, instead of *just*.

9. See, for example, John 12:25; 15:13; 2 Cor. 5:14–15; 1 John 3:16.

10. Elliott Roosevelt and James Brough, *Mother R.* (New York: G. P. Putnam's Sons, 1977). Cited in Mary Ann Glendon, *A World Made New* (New York: Random House, 2001).

CHAPTER 6

1. C. S. Lewis, *Mere Christianity*, rev. and enl. ed. (New York: Harper, 2009), 50.

2. Henry Thoreau, *Where I Lived, and What I Lived For* (1854; London: Penguin UK, 2005).

3. Augustine, *Confessions* (New York: Penguin, 1961), 21.

4. Aristotle, *Nichomachean Ethics*, 2nd ed., trans. Terence Irwin (Indianapolis: Hackett, 1999), 9.

5. John Locke is known for human rights theories such as the idea of "life, liberty, and estate," a theme that came up in several different places in his writing, but specifically stated this way in his *Two Treatises of Government*; John Locke and Peter Laslett, eds. (Cambridge, NY: Cambridge University Press, 1689; 1988), sec. 9, 57, 87, 123, 209, 222.; pp. 101, 325, 341, et al.

6. Thomas Aquinas, *Summa Theologica*, pt. 22, 1a 1ae Q.2 A. 8.

7. C. S. Lewis, *Prince Caspian* (New York: HarperCollins, 1951, 1979), 233.

8. John Piper, *A Hunger for God: Desiring God Through Fasting and Prayer* (Wheaton, IL: Crossway Books, 1997), 10.

9. C. S. Lewis, *The Collected Letters of C .S. Lewis*, vol. 3: *Narnia, Cambridge and Joy 1950–1963* (New York: HarperCollins, 2007), 523.

10. Blaise Pascal, *Pensees* (New York: Penguin, 1966), 74–75.

11. C. S. Lewis, *The Weight of Glory and Other Addresses*, Touchstone ed. (New York: Simon & Schuster, 1996), 26.

CHAPTER 7

1. Khalil Gibran, *Khalil Gibran: The Collected Works* (London: Alfred A. Knopf, 2007), 299.

2. Dallas Willard, *Hearing God: Developing a Conversational Relationship with God* (Downers Grove, IL: InterVarsity Press, 2012), 283.

3. David Konstan, ed. Edward N. Zalta, *The Stanford Encyclopedia of Philosophy*, s.v. "Epicurus" (Fall 2013); http://plato.stanford.edu/archives/fall2013/entries/epicurus. Accessed December 31, 2013.

4. Widely attributed to Epicurus. David Hume most popularly cites Epicurus with this saying in: David Hume, *Dialogues Concerning Natural Religion*, ed. Richard Popkin (Cambridge: Hackett, 1998), 63.

5. C. S. Lewis, *A Grief Observed* (San Francisco: HarperCollins, 1961), 65.

6. Brian Kolodiejchuk, ed., *Mother Teresa: Come Be My Light: The Private Writings of the Saint of Calcutta* (New York: Doubleday, 2007).

CHAPTER 8

1. Evelyn Underhill, *Collected Papers of Evelyn Underhill*, ed. Lucie Menzies (New York: Longmans, Green, 1946), 160.

2. T. S. Eliot, "Shakespeare and the Stoicism of Seneca" (1927), in *Selected Essays*, enlarged ed. (London: 1934), 130.

3. G. K. Chesterton, "On Bright Old Things—and Other Things," in *G.K. Chesterton: Collected Works* (San Francisco: Ignatius, 1990), 473.

4. Blaise Pascal, *Pensees* (New York: Penguin, 1966), 347–48.

5. Augustine, *Confessions* (New York: Penguin, 1961), 169.

CHAPTER 9

1. D. L. Moody, *Notes from My Bible: From Genesis to Revelation* (Chicago: Flemming H. Revell Company, 1895), 141.
2. The Grand Canyon eventually became a national park in 1919.
3. Edmund Morris, "Theodore Roosevelt," *Time*, April 13, 1998, http://www .time.com/time/magazine/article/0,9171,988150,00.html#ixzz1tGxDRzIP. Accessed November 11, 2013.
4. Augustine, "Saint Augustine Quotes and Biography," Quote DB: 1, http:// www.quotedb.com/authors/saint-augustine. Accessed January 3, 2014.
5. An excellent resource that we use at Antioch on this issue is *When Helping Hurts*, by Steve Corbett and Brian Fikkert (Chicago: Moody Publishers, 2009).
6. Augustine, *Homilies on St. John's Epistles*, 7.8.

CHAPTER 10

1. Soren Kierkegaard, *Journals* (London: Oxford University Press, 1939), 117–18.
2. Chad Wellmon, "Why Google Isn't Making Us Stupid . . . or Smart," *Hedgehog Review* 14, no, 1 (Spring 2012), http://www.iasc-culture.org/THR/ THR_article_2012_Spring_Wellmon.php. Accessed December 1, 2013.
3. Johann Georg Heinzmann, *Appell an meine Nation: Über die Pest der deutschen Literatur* (Bern: 1795), 125.
4. A review of Christian Thomasius's *Observationum selectarum ad rem litterariam spectantium* [Select Observations Related to Learning], vol. 2 (Halle, 1702), which was published in the April 1702 edition of the monthly British newspaper *History of the Works of the Learned, Or an Impartial Account of Books Lately Printed in all Parts of Europe*, as cited in David McKitterick, "Bibliography, Bibliophily and Organization of Knowledge," *The Foundations of Knowledge: Papers Presented at Clark Library* (Los Angeles: William Andrews Clark Memorial Library, 1985), 202.
5. Seneca (*Ep. 82.3*), cited in David S. Potter's *A Companion to the Roman Empire* (Oxford: Blackwell Publishing, 2006), 371.
6. Seneca, *Ad Lucilium Epistulae Morales*, vol. 1, trans. Richard M. Gummere (London: William Heinemann, 1917), 7.
7. David Daniels, *The ROI of Video in Email Marketing* (The Relevancy Group, 2013), http://www.streamsend.com/pdf/The_ROI_of_Video_in _Email_Marketing-StreamSend-The%20RelevancyGroup.pdf, 2. Accessed October 10, 2013.
8. Jimmy Daly, "18 Incredible Internet-Usage Statistics," *FedTech* magazine, June 12, 2013, http://www.fedtechmagazine.com/article/2013/06/18 -incredible-internet-usage-statistics. Accessed December 3, 2014.

9. Ibid.

10. Ibid.

11. *Wikipedia*, s.v. "Wikipedia:Modelling Wikipedia's growth," http://en. wikipedia.org/wiki/Wikipedia:Modelling_Wikipedia's_growth ; cf. "File: Enwikipediagrowthcomparison.PNG," http://en.wikipedia.org/wiki/File: Enwikipediagrowthcomparison.PNG. Accessed December 19, 2013.

12. Juliet B. Schor, *The Overworked American: The Unexpected Decline of Leisure* (New York: Basic Books, 1992), 4.

13. In the first *Fantasia* film, music from his ballet *The Rite of Spring* was used in the story about dinosaurs. In *Fantasia 2000*, music from his ballet *The Firebird* was used in the final story about the wood nymph, the elk, and the volcano.

14. Sam Morgenstern, ed., *Composers on Music* (New York: Pantheon, 1956), 442–44, 521–26.

15. "Social Media at Work," Learn Stuff, October 16, 2012, http://www .learnstuff.com/social-media-at-work/. Accessed November 29, 2014.

16. Eyal Ophir, Clifford Nass, and Anthony D. Wagner, "Cognitive control in media multitaskers," *CrossMark* 106, no. 37, http://www.pnas.org/ content/106/37/15583.full?sid=663739be-10dc-4dae-9018-d81525d0e1da. Accessed December 10, 2013.

17. Brother Lawrence, *The Practice of the Presence of God* (n.p.: Kreg Yingst Starving Artist Books, 2008), vii.

18. Brother Lawrence, *The Practice of the Presence of God* (New Kensington, PA: Whitaker House, 1982), 51.

CHAPTER 11

1. Abraham Joshua Heschel, *Man Is Not Alone*, 11–12, in *Abraham Joshua Heschel: Essential Writings*, ed. Susannah Heschel (Maryknoll, NY: Orbis, 2011), 58.

2. C. S. Lewis, *The Voyage of the Dawn Treader* (New York: HarperCollins, 1952), 1.

3. C. S. Lewis, *The Voyage of the Dawn Treader*, 9th printing ed. (New York: MacMillan, 1973), 87.

4. Charles Dickens, *Hard Times* (Bradbury & Evans: London, 1854), 58.

5. *Wikipedia*, s.v. "Chicken" (see "Origins"), http://en.wikipedia.org/wiki/ Chicken#Origins; "Ancient Israelite Cuisine," http://en.wikipedia.org/ wiki/Ancient_Israelite_cuisine#Poultry_and_eggs, s.v. March 11, 2014.

6. Reinhold Niebuhr, *The Essential Reinhold Niebuhr: Selected Essays and Addresses*, Robert McAffe, ed. (New Haven: Yale University Press, 1987), 251.

7. *On Being* radio program, produced by Krista Tippett Public Productions. Copyright ©2007 American Public Media ®

8. *On Being* radio program, produced by Krista Tippett Public Productions. Copyright ©2007 American Public Media ®

9. Matthew Moore, "Stress of modern life cuts attention spans to five minutes," *Telegraph* (UK), November 26, 2008, http://www.telegraph.co.uk/health/healthnews/3522781/Stress-of-modern-life-cuts-attention-spans-to-five-minutes.html. Accessed October 27, 2013.

10. Taylor Hatmaker, "Whoa: Facebook Now Owns Over 25% Of Total Time Spent On Mobile Apps," *rw* (blog), January 23, 2013, http://readwrite.com/2013/01/23/facebook-most-popular-app-comscore?&_suid=13650299170 79009786325553432107. Accessed January 23, 2013.

11. "Social Networking Statistics," Statistic Brain, research date January 1, 2014, http://www.statisticbrain.com/social-networking-statistics/. Accessed December 12, 2013.

12. G. K. Chesterton, "Alarms and Discursions, 1910," in *In Defense of Sanity: The Best Essays of G. K. Chesterton*, eds. Dale Ahlquist, Joseph Pearce, and Aidan Mackey (San Francisco: Ignatius Press, 2011), 103.

13. For a fuller explanation on fast-moving conversations, see my article "Are We Talking Too Fast?" on *HuffPost*'s Religion blog (May 2, 2013), at http://www.huffingtonpost.com/ken-wytsma/are-we-talking-to-fast_b_3201252.html.

14. Reinhold Niebuhr, "Happiness, Prosperity and Virtue," in *The Irony of American History* (Chicago: University of Chicago Press, 1952), 63.

15. A Princeton University study found that in one year (2005), 1.6 million United States church members took mission trips—an average of eight days—at a cost of $2.4 billion. Study by Robert Wuthnow, the Gerhard R. Andlinger professor of sociology at Princeton University, where he is also the chair of the department of sociology and director of the Princeton University Center for the Study of Religion. These numbers are also attested by Rober J. Priest, PhD, professor of mission and anthropology at Trinity Evangelical Divinity School in his January 2008 article in *Missiology* journal, "Service Learning in Short-Term Missions," 53–73.

16. On AskQuestions.tv, Nicholas Wolterstorff tells this story in the video, "The Fine Texture of Justice in Everyday Life." See http://askquestions.tv/dr-nicholas-wolterstorff-the-fine-texture-of-justice-in-everyday-life/.

17. Hal Niedzviecki, *The Peep Diaries: How We're Learning to Love Watching Ourselves and Our Neighbors* (San Francisco: City Lights Books, 2009), 3, 2.

18. Ibid., 30. Here Niedzvieki is speaking of a particular study cited in Jake Halpern's *Fame Junkies* (New York: Houghton Mifflin, 2007).

19. Ibid., 34–35.

20. Henry David Thoreau, "Life Without Principle," in *The Essays of Henry D. Thoreau*, ed. Lewis Hyde (New York: North Point Press, 2002), 198.
21. Henry David Thoreau, *Civil Disobedience and Other Essays*, ed. Philip Smith (New York: Dover, 1993), 84.
22. Reinhold Niebuhr, "Happiness, Prosperity and Virtue," in *The Irony of American History* (Chicago: University of Chicago Press, 1952), 63.
23. C. S. Lewis, *The Lion, the Witch and the Wardrobe* (New York: HarperCollins, 1978).

CHAPTER 12

1. Dietrich Bonhoeffer, *Life Together* (New York: Harper & Row, 1954), 30.
2. C. S. Lewis, *Reflections on the Psalms: The Most Celebrated Musings on One of the Most Intriguing Books of the Bible* (San Diego: Harvest, 1986), 32.
3. "U.S. Religious Landscape Survey: Religious Affiliation," *Pew Forum on Religious and Public Life*, Pew Research Center, February 2008, http://www.pewforum.org/files/2008/02/report-religious-landscape-study-appendixes.pdf. Accessed December 18, 2013.
4. Robert Saucy, *The Church in God's Program* (Chicago: Moody, 1972), 17, 18, 25.
5. C. S. Lewis, *Pilgrim's Regress* (London: Geoffrey Bles, [1933] 1943), 166.
6. Thomas E. Bergler, "When Are We going to Grow Up? The Juvenilization of American Christianity," *Christianity Today*, June 8, 2012, http://www.christianitytoday.com/ct/2012/june/when-are-we-going-to-grow-up.html?paging=off. Accessed November 19, 2013.
7. C. S. Lewis, *The Screwtape Letters* (New York: Touchstone, 1961), 64.

CHAPTER 13

1. J. R. R. Tolkien, *The Lord of the Rings* (New York: HarperCollins Publishers Limited, 2012), Appendix A.
2. C. S. Lewis, *The Pilgrim's Regress* (Grand Rapids: Eerdmans, 1981), 204–5.
3. See G. R. Habermas and J. P. Moreland, *Beyond Death* (Eugene, OR: Wipf and Stock, 2004).
4. A good summary of these varied sets of evidence can be found in chapter 10, "The Evidence from Consciousness: The Enigma of the Mind" in Lee Strobel, *The Case for a Creator* (Grand Rapids: Zondervan, 2004), 247–72.
5. Wilder Penfield, *The Mystery of the Mind* (Princeton, NJ: Princeton Univ. Press, 1975), 79.
6. George MacDonald, *Annals of a Quiet Neighborhood* (New York: Harper & Brothers, 1867), 312. Emphasis in original.
7. Dwight Lyman Moody, "D.L. Moody," Christianity.com, http://www.christianity.com/11528781/. Accessed December 19, 2013.

8. George MacDonald, "Kingship" in *Unspoken Sermons: Series I, II, and III* (Radford, VA: Wilder Publications, 2008), 260.

9. Mark Twain, *Mark Twain's Notebooks and Journals*, vol. 3 (Oakland, CA: University of California Press, 1979), 538 (written May 1889–1890).

10. C. S. Lewis, *The Letters of C.S. Lewis to Arthur Greeves* (22 February 1944), par. 1, p. 501.

11. C. S. Lewis, *The Great Divorce* (Nashville: Broadman & Holman, 1996), 11.

12. Hitler, for example, escaped justice in this life for the atrocities he committed against humanity.

13. For example, in Romans 8:18–21.

14. N. T. Wright, *Surprised by Hope* (New York: Harper One, 2008), 193.

15. Rom. 8:18.

16. 2 Cor. 4:17.

17. 1 Peter 4:13; 5:1; 5:10.

18. Lucian, *The Death of Peregrine*, 11–13, in *The Works of Lucian of Samosata*, trans. H. W. Fowler and F. G. Fowler, 4 vols. (Oxford: Clarendon, 1949), vol. 4. Cited in G. R. Habermas, *The Historical Jesus* (Joplin, MO: College Press, 1996), 206.

CHAPTER 14

1. http://www.catholicnewsagency.com/cw/post.php?id=500. Accessed November 4, 2014.

2. Lynn Hamer, "Bend, Ore. Named 2012 DogTown of the Year," DogChannel.com, August 10, 2012, http://www.dogchannel.com/dogfancy/2012-dogtown-usa.aspx. Accessed December 4, 2013.

3. C. S. Lewis, *The Screwtape Letters* (New York: HarperSanFrancisco, 2001), 37–38.

4. Napoleon Bonaparte, Brainy Quote, http://www.brainyquote.com/quotes/quotes/n/napoleonbo143520.html. Accessed December 19, 2013.

5. Dietrich Bonhoeffer, *Life Together: The Classic Exploration of Faith in Community*, trans. John W. Doberstein (New York: HarperSanFrancisco, 1954), 27.

6. "Desert Fathers" refers to Christian hermits, ascetics, or monastics who lived in the desert (primarily in Egypt) throughout much of the church age.

7. St. John of the Cross, *Dark Night of the Soul*, ed. and trans. E. Allison Peers (New York: Image Books, Double Day Press, 1990), 44.

8. C. S. Lewis, *The Screwtape Letters* (New York: Touchstone, Simon & Schuster, 1996), 41–42.

9. Madeline L'Engle, *Walking on Water: Reflections on Faith and Art* (New York: North Point Press, 1980), 156.

10. Henry Wadsworth Longfellow, *Outre-Mer: A Pilgrimage Beyond the Sea*, vol. 2 (New York: Harper & Brothers, 1835), 4.

11. Cornell West in *Call + Response: A Film About the World's 27 Million Most Terrifying Secrets*, dir. Justin Dillon, Fair Trade Pictures, 2008. Documentary.

12. Walter Brueggemann, "The Costly Loss of Lament" in *The Psalms: The Life of Faith*, ed. Patrick D. Miller (Minneapolis: Fortress Press, 1995), 98–111.

13. Ibid., 102.

14. Ibid., 107.

15. For example, Psalms 33, 96, and 98.

16. See Acts 16.

17. Comments from Alex Mutagubya in this chapter are from a personal interview on October 12, 2013.

18. C. S. Lewis, *The Joyful Christian* (New York: Touchstone, 1996), 98.

19. 2 Cor. 12:9–10.

20. John 15:20.

21. Corrie ten Boom, *The Hiding Place* (Peabody, MA: Hendrickson, 2006), 257.

CHAPTER 15

1. "A Christmas Carol," (Mineola: Dover Publications, 1991), 42.

2. C. S. Lewis, *The Lion, the Witch and the Wardrobe* (New York: HarperCollins, 1978), 118.

3. 2 Peter 3:8 (cf. Psalm 90:4).

4. Thomas Cahill, *The Gifts of the Jews* (New York: Anchor Books, 1998).

5. *Online Etymology Dictionary*, s.v. "grace," http://www.etymonline.com/index.php?term=grace&allowed_in_frame=0. Accessed January 13, 2014.

6. "Cheap grace" is a term first coined and made popular by Dietrich Bonhoeffer in his famous book *The Cost of Discipleship*.

CHAPTER 16

1. This quotation is widely attributed to Kierkegaard, but a closer representation of what Kierkegaard actually said was, "It is perfectly true, as philosophers say, that life must be understood backwards. But they forget the other proposition, that it must be lived forwards." Søren Kierkegaard in Patrick Gardiner's *Kierkegaard: A Very Short Introduction* (Oxford: Oxford University Press, 1988), 95.

2. This assumes, of course, that immoral living leads to a happier life than does taking a more moral approach to life. Pascal did not actually believe this to be true, but assumed it for the sake of the argument.

3. Wendell Berry, "Manifesto: The Mad Farmer Liberation Front" in *The Country of Marriage* (Berkeley: Counterpoint, 2013), 15.

4. "The Deadliest Tsunami in History?" *National Geographic News*, upd. January 7, 2005, http://news.nationalgeographic.com/news/2004/12/1227 _041226_tsunami.html. Accessed December 30, 2013.
5. Matt. 26:36–46.

ABOUT THE AUTHOR

Ken Wytsma is a lover of history and culture, remembers seeing the Allman Brothers Band live in 1995, and can't understand why more people haven't seen the movie *The Shawshank Redemption*. Though he grew up as a strong extrovert, these days you're more likely to find Ken with headphones on in an airplane and in search of a few moments of quiet solitude.

Ken came to faith at age twenty-two at Clemson University and has been on a quest to understand the heart of Christian spirituality ever since. His belief that faith is a lived reality is behind his love for the local church, the value he places in Christian community, and passion for wrestling with the deep questions of life in pursuit of a biblical, authentic, and lived-out Christianity.

A gifted communicator, Ken is known and loved for his transparent and easy style and ability to help others understand their world and faith in new and relevant ways. With degrees in engineering, philosophy, and theology, Ken naturally connects with a broad audience.

Ken is a blogger and writer with articles appearing in *RELEVANT*

Magazine, Church Leaders Top 100, The Huffington Post, Worship Leader Magazine, and more. His first book, *Pursuing Justice: The Call to Live and Die for Bigger Things*, was published in 2012 by Thomas Nelson Publishers.

Ken is the lead pastor of Antioch in Bend, Oregon, which he helped start in 2006. He is also the president of Kilns College, a graduate-only school where he teaches courses on philosophy and justice.

In 2010, along with the creative communities of World Relief and Kilns College, Ken founded The Justice Conference—an annual international gathering that has introduced tens of thousands of men and women to conversations and organizations related to biblical justice.

At the core, Ken is driven by his hope and faith in Christ and believes God is still looking for a few people idealistic enough to think we can change the world—because, as he says, "If God didn't want us to change the world, he wouldn't have asked us to try."

Ken lives in Bend, Oregon with his wife, Tamara, and their four daughters (along with two dogs and four hamsters—all female).

FOR SPEAKING REQUESTS,
VISIT KENWYTSMA.COM

TO ACCESS STUDY GROUP MATERIALS FOR
THE GRAND PARADOX, GO TO
KENWYTSMA.COM/THEGRANDPARADOX